Rediscover Your Family Outdoors

Lloyd and Elsie Mattson

VICTOR BOOKS

a division of SP Publications, Inc.

WHEATON, ILLINOIS 60187

Offices also in Fullerton, California • Whitby, Ontario, Canada • Amersham-on-the-Hill, Bucks, England

Scripture quotations in this book are from the King James Version (KJV), the *New International Version* (NIV), © 1978 by The New York International Bible Society, and the *New American Standard Bible* (NASB), © 1960, 1962, 1968, 1971, 1972, 1973, by The Lockman Foundation, La Habra, California.

Portions of this book are adapted from *Family Camping* by Lloyd Mattson, Moody Press.

Recommended Dewey Decimal Classification: 796.54
  Suggested Subject headings: FAMILY RELATIONS; CAMPING

Library of Congress Catalog Card Number: 80-50003
ISBN: 0-88207-605-1

Contents

Introduction

You can learn much about the concerns of any generation by looking at the books it produced. In the last 20 years of book publication, two topics have been prominent: family life and outdoor recreation. This book attempts to tie the two together.

Our book is written out of anger and love. We're angry at a society that is systematically destroying its citizens with greed, and is peddling moral cancer in our living rooms. But love is stronger than anger. And there is love to be found in relationships with people, especially through family experiences of outdoor adventure.

In this book we share ideas to help other families grow in Christ. We do not suggest that families pack up and move to the country, though some are doing that. We do suggest that people find help in the beautiful world of nature to offset the evil wrought by Satan. While we devote considerable space to the more rugged wilderness trips, we also point out the worth of an afternoon hike or a morning bike ride in the park not far from home.

As families share outdoor experiences together, the basic elements of life become real once again. In a world that seems removed from us, where machines have taken over so many functions, our muscles, minds, and spirits have grown flabby. Some people turn to drugs and electronics to distract them from emptiness and fear. We hope and pray that more families will turn to God's creation in nature and rediscover themselves there.

Lloyd and Elsie Mattson
Duluth, Minnesota
1980

1
Families
That Make It

One pleasant June afternoon we visited Timber Wolf Point Resort near Buyck, Minnesota, a wilderness family vacation center operated especially for Christians. As we talked with the Obergs, owners of the resort, two men and a small boy entered the little store. They needed more minnows.

The boy caught our eye. His hands and face were soiled by chocolate and the miscellaneous occupations of boyhood. His clothing was untidy. But the sparkle in his eye and the wonder he exhibited as he stood with two men, one of them his father, told us that boy was fairly bursting with joy.

Probably, the conversation of the trio who made their way back to their small boat was about the breeze and the lake and the fish. The little guy was reminded that he should let others catch a fish now and then. For these few hours a child felt himself to be a man among men, and that's a good feeling. He was learning secrets through a small adventure; not from planned lectures or Bible studies, but from the lives of his dad and a friend who had thought to include a small boy in their company.

7

The Family—God's Idea

With all options open to Him, God chose to build humanity around family units. Since this is so, we can be certain that everything necessary for wholeness and happiness lies within the family structure. All we have to do is find out how God planned the family to function, then follow His way.

Trouble from the Start

Obviously, it is not easy to find and follow God's plan for families. Right from the beginning something went wrong. The first parents had trouble with their boys, Cain and Abel. And before long, parents were having trouble with each other. God gave Adam one wife but his descendants weren't satisfied with that arrangement.

Ours is not the first generation to suffer from troubled homes. Ever since sin disturbed God's plan for His people, mothers and fathers have known fear and heartache, and children have followed rebellious paths.

Man out of tune with God can never know peace, nor can families who are out of step with God enjoy the delightful harmony He intended. Family troubles today are rooted in the basic problem from which all of mankind's ills flow: sin.

The sin problem follows several paths into the home, and there is no hope that man will at last rid the world of sin and its consequences. But a remedy has been provided that works for families as well as individuals. Is it possible that we have been searching for solutions to family problems in the wrong place?

A Search for Remedies

In writing this book, we do not pose as gurus of some new family success cult. Rather, we hope to be fellow pilgrims in search of the wholeness God has promised in the Person of His Son.

Our search will lead us outdoors, reporting experiences we and others have had in outdoor pursuits. Along the way we will consider reasons why outdoor adventure offers benefits to the family not found in more conventional activities.

We must keep in mind constantly that the remedy for hurting family life must be applied to the innermost depth of the person, not merely wrapped around some hurting member as a soothing poultice. Diversions that temporarily intrigue parents or children accomplish little. Fun all by itself merely postpones the problem. But secrets can be learned in a climate of fun and adventure that may never be discovered elsewhere.

Probably, today's families feel greater pressure than families in past generations have known. But we note with encouragement that a great many young families have determined to succeed in spite of the distractions surrounding our homes. These families are learning that the first line of attack is the spiritual health of Mom and Dad. There is no other way to win.

Movements, decrees, resolutions, and programs all make good contributions to the efforts of families determined to stay together, but the biggest help is the keeping of vows made at the marriage ceremony. People who marry promise to love each other, and love is the fulfillment of all of God's Law. (See Romans 13:10.)

This kind of love transcends feelings and meets the other person's needs without regard to the emotions of the moment. Such a love centers in relationships and reaches beyond one's own family interests to help other families. When casual religion is replaced by New Testament love, fellowship in family and church reaches its highest potential.

Strength from Fellowship
It's hard to imagine a family making it today without the help of a vital Christian fellowship. This too was God's idea. The

idea of the solitary, free-lance Christian does not appear in the New Testament. The church is designed by God to help believers move toward spiritual maturity. The glory of the church is in the strength of its families, not the size of its budget or building.

The family that has determined to succeed will usually seek strength from other families, and not always from those within their particular church. Families, like individuals, take on unique personalities and they feel more comfortable with some friends than they do with others. Without excluding any from sincere friendship, a closer fellowship with a few families provides vital support, and often finds expression through outdoor adventures.

Many young people are shaped more by their friends than by any influence parents can impose or suggest. The same is true, though perhaps in lesser measure, for adults. We become like the people we choose for our friends, and conversely, they become like us.

Friendships do not form on demand. Friendships rarely flourish among people who share common but miserable experiences. But take a group of youth or adults into pleasant experiences and watch friendships bloom!

Early in our career as pastor and wife, we encountered a fellow pastor who somehow rubbed us the wrong way. No doubt the fault lay with us as much as with him, but we simply didn't like one another, and it seemed that we found ourselves on opposite sides in every issue. This troubled us since it was necessary to work with this man in denominational relationships.

We made the tension a matter of prayer, and since we learned a long time ago that the Lord frequently involves His children in the answers to their prayers, we sought for a way to repair this broken relationship. The way came to us when we discovered the pastor had bought a new boat, but lacked opportunity to use it often. Because of our interest in fishing, I invited him to bring his boat to the Paint River for an overnight fishing float trip.

Two days sharing a small boat in a big wilderness accomplished a healing of spirits. Two men, a young pastor and an older pastor, built a friendship that endured for many years. We fished and laughed and cooked dinner on a gravel bar. While rain poured down, we shared a small tent where we talked of light and serious matters, and prayed together.

A simple, friendly initiative opened the way for understanding to flow. How foolish to live with tension, when the joys of friendship are so rewarding! Lasting friendships can be built around good experiences shared with others.

Special Friendships

The most important friendships grow within the family. The greatest reward we have, as we look back on 36 years of marriage, is a close friendship with our five grown children. They are children no longer, but gifted adults leading responsible lives. We meet as peers, but more than that, as friends.

The ultimate family friendship is that which matures between husband and wife when they two make up the household alone. The devastating news of another shattered marriage among middle-aged friends tells you that they failed to cultivate friendship. They were mates, producing children, and staying together because of social pressures. When they were again alone they discovered that they didn't really like each other. Since society has become more tolerant of divorce, another couple parted.

A small family camping area in western Pennsylvania became a place of healing for a middle-aged couple whose marriage had fallen apart. They had never taken the time to build common interests, but drifted along after the family was raised until small tensions grew beyond control. Counseling and repeated efforts accomplished little and they decided on divorce.

A friend suggested that they should spend one last weekend together sharing in an informal family camping retreat. Arrangements were made to surround the troubled couple with supportive, understanding friends in the campsite. No one lectured them and only a few knew their plight. The couple simply observed others about their age who had a joyful marriage after their children were gone. Soon, they began to see their problems as trivial expressions of selfishness, rooted in spiritual immaturity. Through quiet conversation with a neighbor camper, they squared their lives with the Scriptures.

We asked what reasons they could give for the renewing of their love for each other and the Lord, when repeated visits to counselors and Christians back home had failed. They weren't quite sure; however, away from the familiar surroundings of their home where so much bitterness had been expressed, and in the company of Christians who seemed completely happy in mature marriages, they felt maybe their marriage could survive.

For that couple, a weekend retreat in a borrowed camper began to heal their marriage.

Carefully planned outdoor recreation provides opportunity for friendships to grow among family members and with other families. It also offers potential for children to form helpful friendships with other Christian youth and for adults to find strength in the company of other adults facing common concerns.

Pleasant experiences shared together strengthen friendships and build happy memories. A fortune in the bank can't buy rich memories—or good friends.

A Christian Home—What Is It?

We should establish what we mean by a Christian family. What defines a home as "Christian"? There is a home of our acquaintance where they did everything that was supposed to be right. The father had turned to Christian work, Sundays found the family in church, morning and evening, and prayer meetings were faithfully attended. They had regular family devotions, including a hymn, extended Bible reading, homily, and prayer. They legislated dress styles, hair lengths, and music. Violations of the law were summarily punished.

Yet the evening we visited that home, we learned that one son was a runaway and in jail. The younger son was so mean we dared not let him out of our sight lest he hurt our children. Something was wrong.

Not every family that attends church faithfully maintains a Christian home. Not every family made up of Christian people exhibits Christian qualities in the home, for many followers of Christ live far beneath their spiritual potential. A family of troubled Christians living under the same roof is not likely to stumble by accident upon the secret of a Christian home.

For our purposes we will consider that home to be Christian where parents determine for each family member to grow to Christian maturity, and where they develop a strategy for carrying out their determination. This strategy is accorded priority over all other considerations.

A Christian Home—Can It Stand the Test?

This kind of home faces severe temptations. Social custom is one. The old American tradition of getting ahead is another. Who questions the propriety of hard work, frugality and self-improvement? You don't get promotions by taking time off for camping trips! Many a man has spent himself building a business, and spent his wife and children at the same time. He may be widely heralded as a model Christian businessman, successful and wealthy. His generous tax-deductible gifts are coveted. But his comfortable retirement brings no comfort as he reflects on the years he lost when his children were small. Dollars don't buy pleasant memories!

Even the church can tempt the parent who would give priority to the spiritual needs of the family. The same qualities that help a person become a good mother or father make for effective church leadership. Since the supply of able and willing leaders is low, the pressure rests upon the few to give many evenings to committees, studies, and program leadership. How can anyone say No to God's work?

Well, Paul had a word to say about the qualifications for leadership. Those who failed to have their children under control were disqualified. And anyone who failed to provide for his own house was declared to be worse than an infidel. Surely that provision reached beyond food and lodging. The Christian family will be given the wisdom to know what God expects both in business and in church life, so that they can care for each other's needs.

Here's a rule of thumb you can follow, if you are determined to maintain a Christian home. God never demands service in one area of life that causes us to fail Him in another.

It seems a fair assertion that God would never lead a person into a responsibility that would cause him or her to neglect the family. This does not mean that some Christian homes will not be irregular. The father's job may cause him to travel, perhaps for extended periods of time. But parents can compensate by creating new ways to fulfill the needs of the children.

This was put to the test in our lives through 15 years of executive and field work, some of them while the children were still at home. The load was extra heavy on Elsie, but priority was given to making the kids feel part of our ministry. Each youngster was included in working trips, often by air, where he would find some enjoyment. And the summer program included the entire family as much as they cared to share in it.

On several occasions, invitations or assignments would come for work in Christian camps that had a no-family policy for staff people. Sometimes these camps had no accommodations for family members, or unfortunate experiences in the past had rendered staff families unwelcome.

When I notified the camp that I felt it necessary to include all or some of my family on summer assignments, there was considerable fuss. Why should I demand to be an exception to the rule? I replied simply that I need not be an exception. They had the liberty to recruit someone else for the job. But since I was away from home frequently when the kids were in school, I could accept only those summer appointments where they could come along. We agreed, of course, to cover their expenses and secure family housing when that was necessary.

Many of the anecdotes you read in these pages grew out of summer assignments that included the family. And there were occasions when an assignment was withdrawn.

Personal interests and ambitions can preclude spiritual vitality in some homes. Father's or mother's social or recreational interests can be so compelling that little time remains for family life. Dad may be vital to the shop bowling team, Mother may be the best P.T.A. chairperson the school ever had. Either Mom or Dad may have close friends that simply must be given time. Even the compulsion to keep a tidy house or trim lawn can destroy any hope for a Christian home.

How so? Well, there's no way to have a Christian home without working at it and giving the process time. Lots of time. Much has been written about quality time versus quantity, and appropriately so. But only the other person, child, or mate can determine the quality of the time.

I will never forget one special evening. It happened by a small lake in Alaska in company with our fourth child, a son. The evening was beautiful and trout were rising on the lake. The tent was pitched and supper was simmering on the fire. It was an eight-year-old's dream. Suddenly he said, "You know, Dad, this is the first time you and I have ever been out alone ... just us."

I didn't know that. The thought had never occurred to me.

A Christian Home—A Last Hope?

The Christian home is the last and best hope for parents and children. Let us call that home *Christian* where the spiritual and friendship needs of each family member are given priority. Such a home will establish its own criteria for success, allowing neither the business, social, nor religious world to intrude. This determination is based on an assumption that meeting the spiritual needs of family members is God's first charge to parents, and that He never demands anything that will cause them to fail in that charge.

Let's look at some of the factors common to our day that make the Christian home the last hope for youth and adults, and that make outdoor adventure the most promising alternative for families striving for closeness.

The agrarian society has long since passed, when families worked together to survive. While we may idealize those days, few would choose to return to them. Urban life prevails even in the country today, for the wonders of electronics bind the whole world together with ever tightening cords.

The theme of leisure brought by industrialization and higher wages has been discussed widely. Cars and good roads have brought instant mobility to anyone old enough to secure a driving license. With family mobility now a life-shaping influence, and one fourth of all families moving each year, the multigenerational household is hard to find. The wisdom and example of godly grandparents on a day-by-day basis has been lost to most children, as has the sense of family discipline that grows when more than parents and children share a household.

Society in general seems to be turning increasingly toward self-fulfillment as the ultimate good. This and the loss of moral moorings have opened the door to a public evil unthinkable just a few years ago. Situation ethics and permissiveness leave many young people without guidelines.

If you wonder if this judgment is too harsh, scan your daily newspaper or a national magazine, and evaluate what you read. Pause at the entertainment sections and note what is playing at the movie houses and on television. Look at the newsstand and drive slowly past the porno row in your city.

"But I protect my home from these evils," you say. Maybe, but you cannot protect family members from the influence societal evil has on friends in school or office. Nor can you completely shield your children or yourself from the pervasive sweep of the media. Most of us are bombarded many hours a day with sights and sounds that dull our moral sensitivities.

We cannot withdraw from the world. Living in some remote Christian commune that barred all news from the world would frustrate God's plan that we be salt and light to people who don't know Christ.

How then can we save our children and ourselves from these negative influences of society? We can build loyalties to God's Word and His ways through the determined building of a Christian home. We can teach the Scriptures in a real-life setting, both by precept and example. We can help our kids find Christian friends, and we can create occasions when we can draw away for a time from the noise and glare and find tranquility in the world of nature which God made for man to enjoy.

In the pleasant environment of the outdoors, many good things can happen to people, and this we will consider in the pages that follow. But first let's look more closely at the forces that oppose our efforts to grow in Christ.

2
The World, the Flesh, and the Devil Come Home

Sin did not originate with the movie camera or high speed color press. No new sins have been created in the past century. Family problems have been around as long as mankind has existed. You need only read the Old Testament to learn this. But new factors introduced in this century have caused problems of a magnitude never before experienced in history.

An expanded leisure and affluence have created a market for the vast entertainment industry. Today our national heroes and heroines are entertainers, and the roles they play not only reflect, but shape society.

Certainly, good books and plays exist, but they do not generally receive the attention that the less wholesome ones do.

The World

The Apostle John wrote, "Do not love the world or anything in the world" (1 John 2:15), and the Apostle Paul spoke of the world when he penned his classic passage, "I urge you, brothers, in view of God's mercy, to offer yourselves as living sacrifices, holy and pleasing to God—which is your spiritual worship. Do not conform any longer to the pattern of this world, but be transformed by the renewing of your mind. Then you will be able to test and approve what God's will is—His good, pleasing and perfect will" (Rom. 12:1-2). This is the world under Satan's dominion, the world that crucified Jesus.

While all of nature is affected by the entrance of sin into the world, the natural world appears to be affected less than areas which call for human choice. It is into this outdoor world that we often retreat to balance the influences of society which so frequently oppose what we believe is God's will.

However, this retreat is not for our survival as Christians. We have been assured a way to survive, and that is through the power of God's Spirit living in the hearts of Jesus' followers. The Bible does not teach that Christians are to be carried along by some mystic force to heaven. True faith begets action, and active discipling is a lifelong process that leads toward spiritual maturity. The occasional retreat, then, to the world of nature, is for our personal benefit and that we might better serve God in society.

There is a cherished spot in Wyoming where our family has spent parts of several summers. Blind Bull Creek is near there, and Bailey Lake, and the swift-flowing Greys River with its cutthroat trout. There we met Sam and Ila of the Box Y Ranch. These friends have now sold the ranch but have retained five acres and built a snug cabin on the river.

One fall I borrowed a few days in the midst of a trip to breathe a little mountain air. Life grows awfully stuffy if you don't take time off to breathe now and then. Sam met me at the Jackson airport and we drove to the ranch in his pickup.

One golden afternoon, Sam joined me to help me find that mule deer buck I'd come for. We topped a low hill in the foothills of the Wyoming Range and sat scanning the far side of the valley. No deer showed itself and we just relaxed, enjoying the glory of autumn in the hills. As the sun was dropping behind us, the aspen turned the hills to gold with scarlet flashes of sumac. We sat in silence.

Finally Sam spoke, "Reverend, a man don't live a lifetime in these hills without he gets something in his heart from the Lord." Sam had got part of God's message, and I shared with my friend as best I could the rest of the story, about Jesus and His unique provision for rescuing people from sin and condemnation. The outdoors does have something to say to those who will take time to listen.

Sacred VS Secular?

In religious circles there has been a dreadful dichotomy purporting the unbiblical idea that all life is divided into two parts, the sacred and the secular. That which lies within the bounds of the religious has spiritual worth. All else is either evil or neutral. Fun is secular, unless it results from games in the church parlor or a humorous evangelist. The church bowling league barely qualifies. To equate with the sacred a family on an all-day hike, won't do in the minds of some people.

But God is not chained in church while the family goes camping. Nor does God view His children differently when they are playing than He does when they are praying. We are equally His at every moment of life, and when we gain this concept we are not tempted to feel guilty when we plan hours of family fun rather than planning some "spiritual" exercise.

A theology of expediency nourishes this dichotomy. This theology declares that what is good for the leader's program is God's best for the follower. The perfect attendance pin is this heresy's badge. You may miss three Sundays because of illness and still win the pin, but you will surely grieve the Lord and the superintendent if you're absent by reason of a family camping trip!

The drive for perfect attendance is patently a device to build the average attendance of the group and may be promoted as a higher good than any personal family interest. Church leaders have been known to use theological force to intimidate the faithful and further their own institutional aims. And in so doing, they may undervalue the concept of the priesthood of the believer.

Happily, we seem to be moving away from this viewpoint and toward the trusting, wholesome thought that a Christian father still functions as spiritual leader of his family, and that worship and prayers by a forest stream are as acceptable to God as those offered in church.

We do *not* propose that families become gypsies, roaming constantly about the countryside, ignoring the privileges of the church fellowship. We do suggest that occasions will arise when one or several families will become the church in the wilderness, a company of God's people worshiping the Creator God away from their brothers and sisters back home.

One of the happiest Sunday morning worship congregations we ever shared met around picnic tables along a lake in northern Minnesota. The whole church had gone camping, and a sign on the church door back in town said so. Initially, a few church members had made quite a fuss when the pastor proposed the idea. They'd felt that it just wasn't proper to close the church on Sunday.

The pastor pointed out that the church wasn't a building but people. And that the church would worship as it did every week. Only the sanctuary would change. The plan was announced well in advance. Rides were provided for all who did not care to camp out Saturday night. A notice on the church door gave the location of the morning worship.

The great majority of participants found the weekend to be a highlight of the year. It seemed to me that the values gained by families who camped together outdoors for three days, some for two, far outweighed any possible loss suffered by a break with tradition. The earliest churches had no buildings, you remember. They met in homes, sometimes by a river, and later in caves. We do not doubt that God met with them.

The philosophies and values of the world call your family with a piercing, strident voice. You cannot completely muffle the sound. Once a Christian could simply stay away from objectionable places but television changed all that. You may choose to do without TV, and many families make that choice. Yet television dominates the lives of people and its echoes are heard in the influence television has on its multitude of addicts.

This influence cannot be missed. On a lovely autumn weekend, we were privileged to minister to 100 junior-high young people representing a dozen evangelical churches. All but a handful who shared the retreat were life-long Sunday School members and most came from solid Christian homes. They knew the songs and choruses and they could quote the right Bible verses. Most could confess a personal faith in Christ, naming the time and place of conversion. No doubt the majority were baptized church members.

Thinking to gain evaluations of the retreat from the campers, we called for testimonies during the final program. An awkward, embarrassed silence persisted for some minutes. Someone whispered, "They're just shy."

To get them talking, I asked, "What's your favorite TV show?" The response was instantaneous and prolonged. The young people shouted out the names of their favorites. The loudest favored the current sexy police show featuring three women in a weekly series of sensual episodes.

What troubled us most was the apparent indifference toward

the episode displayed by adult leaders of the retreat. They seemed to be amused, and gave no evidence that they felt anything alarming had occurred. The voice of the world is loud, and sins of the flesh are accepted as common fare for the citizenry, in books, films, conversations, and too often in personal behavior.

Great numbers of America's teens are sexually active. Venereal disease sweeps in epidemic proportions through our cities and towns. Teen pregnancies are common. We need not dwell on pornography with its deadly grip on minds both young and old.

Spinning off the sins of the flesh are abortion, easy divorce, the common acceptance of live-in friends. But what is most serious is that we have lost much of our sensitivity to evil, in society, and even in the church.

Test Your Home

Again we must ask if this judgment is too harsh. Test the spiritual climate and moral sensitivity in your own heart and home. How often do you turn off offensive programs? Consider the plight of young, undisciplined minds, which are so impressionable.

The problem with sensual pleasure outside of marriage is that it can decline into perversion and sadism. Man's appetites are so soon satiated he must devise new and grosser forms of evil in order to find amusement. And beyond that lies emptiness and despair.

Sadder yet is to observe the effect on children when parents take no positive action to counteract the world's influence by providing alternative models of life. Some years ago we visited a home that had been recently built by a Christian family. The house was lovely and the decor reflected fine tastes.

However, a mid-teen son's room betrayed a frightening lack

in that home. His room was decorated with all the symbols of the day. Photos of TV stars decorated the walls, mostly women in suggestive poses. Glued to the ceiling directly over his bed was a huge poster of the current TV sex symbol dressed in a bikini. The record jackets identified his taste in music. Somehow the Bible on' his desk seemed out of place. What troubled us most was the sly smile of the boy's mother as she commented glibly on the strange tastes of young boys.

In contrast we visited another new home and enjoyed a guided tour. The decor was not overtly religious but you could not mistake the Christian tone of life. This family too had a son, not quite 12. His room was simple—a few books, a few sports items, a small stereo. The music we heard in his room was similar to what we heard on the stereo in the living room. The tastes and life of a boy were being shaped by the examples of his parents.

One home neglected to suggest any alternative to what their son would hear through the media and see on the living room TV. The other family made good music a part of everyday life. The results were evident in the boys. Thinking Christians know the effect of evil or banal input on their children, from the incredibly effective sights and sounds of the media.

Our children cannot escape the stimuli of sensual entertainments, nor the powerful influence of friends who have little or no discipline in their homes. It is not enough simply to forbid; we must provide alternatives to the world's pleasures, and we must teach God's way toward wholeness of the spirit. And we dare not leave the task to the church alone!

The world and the flesh are, of course, simply expressions of that ancient, dark conflict between God and Satan. The world God made was good: "And God saw everything that He had made, and, behold, it was very good" (Gen. 1:31). Then the world became the battlefield as Satan challenged man's loyalty to the Creator. Nothing has been the same for man since.

If we seek solutions to family problems primarily through sociology or education, we will fail. Apart from the redeeming work of Christ there will be no lasting benefits, for Satan cares little how respectable we become as long as we fall short of a saving, renewing faith. Once reliable social institutions such as public schools and community organizations rarely support the Christian ethic. However, this is no excuse for Christian lethargy in the community. There are battles to be fought, whether over textbooks, pornography, or public decency.

And while we will not fully defeat evil in the world, we, His people, can claim total victory through Christ in our hearts. This is the victory we seek through family times together in the outdoors.

We make no claim that outdoor adventure alone will win the battle, but we do believe that families who share pleasant hours together have a great advantage over those who rely solely on traditional programs related to our formal religious life.

We believe parents have a duty to provide extended times together for friendships to grow and for memories to gather. They can create opportunities for the truths of Scripture to penetrate young hearts, as children see God's love modeled in their parents during shared outdoor experiences.

3
Meeting the Real Needs

Family wholeness is built around three kinds of relationships. Parents relate to each other as husband and wife, and as mutually responsible parents of children. There is the parent-child relationship, and finally, the sibling relationship. Outdoor adventure offers several distinct advantages for strengthening all these relationships.

The exceptional family, that is the one child or one parent family, or the multigenerational family, will face challenges that are somewhat different, but the principles for family wholeness are much the same as those that apply to the family of Mom, Dad, and the kids.

Dad's Needs

A teenage boy talked with us following a campfire discussion one evening. "If only once my dad would admit he was wrong, maybe we could get along." That boy had a problem, but his father had a bigger problem. Pity the man who must always be right! A man needs to know that he is still growing. In order to do that he must take risks, become vulnerable, and share life on common terms with his family. A family camping trip helps to accomplish this.

1. Men need to discover their children. Many men retreat from the basic responsibility for raising their children, right after they are born. The demands of career, church, and community give them an alibi for turning the care of the children over to the mothers. Such fathers can go for weeks without a positive, friendly encounter with the children, especially as they enter adolescent years. Shared outdoor activity places a father in a different role than he often assumes in the home. The chances are good that he will see his children differently too.

Many men need a change of setting to rediscover their wives. The strength of the bond between husband and wife is the force that holds the family together. Much has been made of the wife's submission to the headship of the husband, according to Paul's instructions to the Ephesians (Eph. 5:22-33). Less has been heard about the awesome charge to husbands, to love as Christ loved. Outdoor activity away from the home, so often seen as the woman's domain, provides man the opportunity to rediscover his wife and practice the loving headship God requires.

Men need to show active leadership in the family. Of necessity home duties must be delegated, and the children generally see Mother in this decision-making role. However, when the family goes camping, the father does not drive off to work. He stays around to arbitrate differences and apply discipline as needed. He faces such questions as, "How does this tent go up?"

2. Men need to discover themselves. Sheer pride keeps many men from spiritual growth. They reject the thought that they have problems, or that they are neglecting family members. A man can easily rationalize his attitudes and busyness. Whatever most highly motivates a man, is probably also the greatest danger to his own spirit. When a man dares to break away for time in the outdoors, there is a good possibility that the jarring noise of life will subside enough for him to hear God's voice.

3. *Man needs to obey the Lord.* Whatever problems a family may encounter, the husband as head of the family is ultimately responsible to work out the solution. One valuable tool for preventive maintenance in family life is shared outdoor adventure.

Mom's Needs

The current change in social custom and philosophy of life threatens the serenity of many wives. The feminist movement raises questions about the worth of her role as wife and mother. Materialism as a basic doctrine of life—or in many cases the fact of inflation—forces wives to seek jobs in order to keep pace with rising costs. A whole industry is growing in order to accommodate working mothers, the business of day care centers. Occasional outdoor adventure can help meet a desperate need in the heart of a working mother, a need to spend unbroken hours and days with her family. The mother who is home needs time away just as much. A sensitive husband will recognize that she needs a break from home routine. Family outings will provide that for her, with as much of the work load as possible passing to the husband and children.

Whatever happened to family fun with husbands and wives enjoying each other and their children? The competitive spirit that seems to dominate most of life has crept into the home. It's time to play down competition and elevate participation for the sheer joy of shared pleasure. Outdoor adventure can help husbands and wives meet deep needs if they recognize these needs and work at them. Mothers and fathers need to grow in Christ.

The Kids' Needs

We have considered some of the perils young people face as they live in a morally bankrupt society. Parents everywhere agonize over the future of their families. However, within this troubled world there are also many good things, and children need to discover them. But unless the parents create opportunities for discovery, it is unlikely the children will.

We will say quite often that outdoor adventure is but one option available to families for enriching the lives of their children. Many wholesome interests can be pursued in the arts, sports, community life and the church. The outdoors will appeal to many as a worthy place for discovering the good life.

Children need a place to grow, to gain new experiences and to exercise initiative. We all tend to live vicariously, with very little personal involvement in producing the material essentials of life. This personal need for new encounters lies at the heart of several problems children face.

We smile at the report of a parent who yelled to her noisy children upstairs, "Whatever you're doing, stop it!" This is the attitude we sometimes take toward children. We have so little to offer that is constructive, challenging, or fun. With proper planning, outdoor adventure can become all three.

Probably, a child's deepest need is to see Christ in the lives of his or her parents. A little child especially needs to feel close, and gain the warmth of God's love from his parents. Whatever values a child may gain from the church or community, nothing can replace cherished hours and days of meaningful association with Mother and Father.

Children need models in godliness. Paul wrote, "I urge you to imitate me" (1 Cor. 4:16). The imitation of a winsome example is far easier than bringing doctrine to life. Youth generally mirror the adults who mean the most to them. Real character surfaces when families work and play together in the outdoors, for there is no escape to the office or shop.

Children need to play. This seems too obvious to discuss, but a deep truth can be overlooked. Children do not want parents to enter their fantasies, but they do want to share in experiences that are fun for both parents and themselves. We need to enter the children's world sincerely, to enjoy what they are enjoying. Dads once worked and built and fished with their sons. Mothers baked and looked after a litter of kittens with their children. Life brought families together in activities each person found pleasant. We don't find much of that around the neighborhood anymore. Outdoor adventure can recover this quality of life for the family.

Children need to learn to get along with each other. Sibling squabbles seem to be an inevitable fact of family life. But need this be so? Scrapping generally arises when kids can think of nothing better to do. Their motivation arises partly from a secret game called, "Let's-see-how-mad-we-can-make-Mom-and-Dad." A variation is, "Let's-see-who-can-get-the-most-attention." Active, enduring and enjoyable outdoor activities can help focus energies elsewhere than on sibling squabbles.

Family Needs

A family is more than the sum of its members, just as a husband and wife are more than two people living together. A family takes on personality. Within the family flow energies with amazing potential for good or evil. When one member exploits the family for personal gain, the whole family suffers. When the family shares activities of common pleasure, all the members grow toward wholeness.

The deep joy of a spirit set free in Christ is what makes the family a joyous, thriving body. To accomplish this, the family must be honest, and this demands vulnerability and humility of spirit. Certainly, you can find occasions for humility in the outdoors, and few things render one so vulnerable as a stormy night in a crowded camper!

The small privacies we take for granted at home are forfeited when the family shares a tent, trailer, or crowded cabin. Family members learn to respect each other's needs and to limit personal freedom. Weak points in the family fabric are soon exposed, allowing repair work to begin.

A hunting companion once looked in dumbfounded awe at his partner who had suggested that the two should spend the night in the woods without shelter or food in order to be in good game territory at dawn. It was totally inconceivable to him that a person could do without food, improvise a shelter, or spend a night without light and risk harm from wild beasts.

Of course there was no danger from beasts, nor any risk to health, either from the chilly night or the lack of a meal. But a city-bound spirit could not imagine surviving without gadgets and the amenities money could provide.

Whether the need for actual survival ever arises or not, a person gains a sense of well-being when he or she has learned how to survive. This can be accomplished through experience in the outdoors.

Families need to develop self-reliance and initiative. There is no better place than the wilderness to gain these qualities. And there are no better teachers than parents who are determined to equip their children for life.

4
Steps Toward Outdoor Adventure

Some years ago we read in a newspaper about a Chicago boy who had never seen a live tree. A short bus ride in any direction would have carried the lad along tree-lined boulevards and into parks with great trees growing everywhere. Thousands of acres of forest preserves wandered into the heart of the city. Still the boy had never seen a tree.

How could that happen? Well, the boy lived in a walk-up apartment with many brothers and sisters. His tired, discouraged mother had no time for unnecessary bus rides. The school, the store, and the neighborhood theater were all within easy walking distance of the boy's home. The streets served as his park and playground. A boy can survive without seeing a tree. He probably never thought about it until some reporter picked up on the idea for a story.

It's possible there are a multitude of kids who have missed the basic joys of nature because their parents are preoccupied with the affairs of daily life. Neither the kids nor their parents give much thought to knowing about birds and trees and rivers. Their losses are significant all by themselves, for people who lack an appreciation for God's good world are greatly impoverished in spirit. But there is an even greater loss.

The outdoors offers a unique environment for discovery and spiritual growth within the family. Living for God demands much more than physical survival. A child deserves to see a tree now and then.

Barriers to Discovery

Preoccupation is a major barrier to outdoor adventure in many families. Life is demanding and many diversions exist that require far less effort from the parents than packing the car for a camping trip. Life can become cluttered for all families who are involved in the church, the school, and the community, as well as in their work.

The clutter affects children and youth as well as parents. The days are too few and too short to get everything done.

Inertia is the cousin of preoccupation. Even when a family senses trouble because of the clutter and the negative input creeping in from many sources, they lack the energy to break out of the web. Outdoor interests of earlier years are only warm memories, and outdoor skills have been almost forgotten.

Also there's the cost factor. Dollars are shrinking, costs are swelling, energy is scarce, and a family has so many other needs. Outdoor adventure always seems to call for equipment and gas money, camping fees, and special clothing. As good stewards, should the family take up a form of recreation that will further strain the budget?

And what about the little ones? They surely can't go camping. Little kids need sanitary surroundings and regular hours. They might get hurt in the woods, and the bugs are bad. Mom and Dad aren't sure they want to move off the patio either. Why put the family under pressure when the children are so young?

There can be a powerful religious argument against activity that lures the family out of town. Would not the time and money be better invested in spiritual pursuits? How can one serve the Lord if he is off on some lake or river, or chasing about the mountains, or biking along a country lane?

When all other barriers are hurdled, one remains. . . . *One of these days we'll get at it.* The bikes hang in the garage, the tent lies rolled up in the attic. The tackle box gathers dust in the basement. *But one of these years we'll get out there again. It's really great to go camping, and we're going to go . . . soon.* Meanwhile, there are kids who never see trees, or cows, or mountains.

Avenues to Discovery

Parents are confronted with choices every day. Some of these choices have eternal consequences, and if choices are made only on the basis of convenience, the years will slip away forever.

How often Elsie and I sit in our comfortable living room and enjoy letters from our grown kids. We still can't understand how the years slipped by so fast! There's a dad out there who would swap every committee he ever sat on for a few more memories of fishing with his sons. He is grateful that there are times to remember, but there could have been more. The kids have made it all right, and they never complain of neglect. It's Dad who laments over the honorable trivia that so cluttered his life that he didn't have time for the kids.

Making choices takes courage, especially when some good things have to be discontinued in order to do better things.

The daily paper ought to prod us out of our inertia; or perhaps a visit to the local drug treatment center, or the disco on a Saturday night will wake us up. Or perhaps a stroll through pornography row will shake us parents to action. The cities agonize over kids stupefied by booze and drugs; over unwed teen mothers and diseased youth; teen prostitution, and profligate sex encouraged by nightly TV shows. Perhaps outdoor adventure will not be a major activity for our homes, but without some aggressive action we're almost certain to lose.

We are continually making choices about how we will spend our money. Investment in character and spiritual vigor is far more lasting than houses, land, cars, and gadgets. And infinitely more lasting than money in the bank. When we close down our houses to go camping, we consume very little more energy than we would in normal home life. If we go biking or backpacking or canoeing, we come out ahead!

Caring parents plan all activities according to the capabilities and needs of little ones. But don't underestimate the kids! Early and pleasant exposure to the outdoors is the best assurance you can have that a love for nature will grow. Children generally reflect the attitudes of parents, at least during the early years. Blessed is the grandfather who takes his grandkids fishing before they start school.

Watching the joy on the face of a child riding behind Dad on a bike is an answer for those who would protect a youngster from wind and dust. Germs and exposure are not the perils that destroy youth today.

A narrow theology that sees some spiritual compromise in nonreligious activity is not based on the Bible. We recall the statement concerning Jesus as a Boy, that He grew in every dimension of personality: mind, body, spirit, and social relationships. Is He not our example? When children discover that all of life is sacred, that they are equally God's in every moment of life, they are moving toward spiritual maturity.

Hopefully, some bolt of conscience will jar the procrastinator from his perch. The barriers to action exist primarily in the minds and lethargy of people who suffer hypothermia of the spirit. No matter how hard it is to get moving, the alternatives are worse. Spiritual death lurks nearby for our children.

Begin to Plan

You can begin to plan simple outings not far from your home. The values of outdoor adventure do not grow out of some special place, but from the relationships kids and parents develop while doing enjoyable things together. Most of what we learn we gain through no conscious effort. Who taught you to talk? You heard words and struggled to duplicate them. Love, kindness, laughter, prayer, respect, worship; a child imitates these too when they become expressions of the life of a parent.

Collect simple outdoor gear. A cane pole in hand is worth 10 fly rods to come someday. The best trips are often the simplest. Way back in memory there's a dad and a lad walking across a field in search of acorns. A hundred hikes in rugged mountains from Alaska to Maine blend into a montage of memory, but that autumn day remains single and clear. And the boy was just about three. The giving of self is worth far more than the fanciest gear in the West.

These are seed thoughts for parents who are considering a change in family direction. Before we look at specific kinds of adventure, we should consider the art of family worship. Worship is an art, not a technique. While we are God's persons equally at all times, in worship we bring our thoughts to focus on Him as a Person.

Worship and Discovery

The term "Family Worship" conjures up a specter of Father reading a long passage from a huge Bible while Mother prays for the missionaries. Or possibly the scene finds someone reading hastily from a small booklet, struggling with the big words. For many Christian homes, the term simply generates guilt, for these families never got around to any regular pattern for family devotions.

Families that enjoy happy, meaningful worship will carry their practice into the outdoors with no break in the cadence of the day. Worship, being an art, does not require any special format or special setting.

But many families have never managed to organize their time or schedules to get everyone together for devotions. A prayer before meals must do.

Before there can be family worship, there must be parents who walk with God. It will not do to slip a mystic prayer shawl over one's head for devotions, then remove it and revert to one's usual, casual self. It's not too difficult to establish a ritual, but it's of little value when it is only ritual. The worship that reaches a child's heart is the overflow from the heart of a loving Christian.

When parents plan family worship, they would do well to think back to their feelings about worship when they were small. What meaning did the reading and praying have? A good memory is one of the sharpest tools for building family worship.

Worship is an awareness of God's loving presence accompanied by praise and thanksgiving. The spirit exults with the psalmist, "Bless the Lord, O my soul: and all that is within me, bless His holy name" (Ps. 103:1). The challenge that the family faces is to develop worship patterns that will bless the child's heart.

God made Himself real when He approached people. Israel was granted the pillar of cloud and fire. Moses had a burning bush. An angel appeared to Abraham. Jesus came as the God-man, revealing the Father to humanity. How can we make spiritual truth real to children? We can follow Jesus' example and tell stories.

Surely, we need printed helps for daily devotions. But why not bring the prophets and apostles along on your outings? Don't hesitate to tell the old familiar Bible stories. David and Goliath have many miles left in them. Elijah on Mt. Carmel wins every time.

The quiet reading of a Bible story, a few minutes of conversation about the story, perhaps a song or two that everyone knows, then prayer about real people and real needs—this is family worship. There is no need to read a homily, or to preach. Worship should focus on God, not on the clock or on a known ritual.

Sometimes, a longer worship time is appropriate, especially when camping with several families, or when the purpose for a trip includes training in private worship. Chapter 10 includes an approach to worship that utilizes the Bible story as a basis for Bible discovery, personal devotions, and group sharing. The plan is explained and guidelines are supplied for the devotional leader and campers. Ideas may be gleaned for building family or larger group worship for outings.

Generally, our worship fails, not because we offer too little but because we attempt too much. One concept understood is worth 1000 ideas endured. The "Trail Devotions" in chapter 10 present one key verse for each day, drawn from a Bible story. Worship and sharing for the day centers in that verse and story. One suggestion that might prove useful for family devotions is the book *Pray Back*. It teaches youngsters how to respond in prayer to God's Word.

As you plan for outdoor adventure, consider the devotional values of Sunday worship. When circumstances allow, you will enrich your family by dropping in at a nearby church.

Our route toward Alaska one summer took us through a

small mining town in Wyoming. We found no campground for the night, but paused on a knoll to prepare supper. On the edge of the town, we saw a small white church. As we completed our meal, several cars drove into the churchyard. We thought perhaps a prayer meeting was about to begin.

Thinking that we could gain directions to a camping area, we joined the prayer group. What a delightful evening! Our son brought his guitar along and sang for the people. They seemed so pleased that strangers would drop in to share their service. From the church we went to a home where a lad was confined with a serious injury. We sang and fellowshiped more. We found that our coming gave a lift to the people who were passing through difficult days. And as a bonus, we were invited to be guests in the pastor's home for the night. The Alaska camping trip held many adventures, but none of them are remembered with greater joy than our Thursday evening visit with brothers and sisters in Christ.

Just as your worship grows out of the heartfelt attitude of faith, joy, and love, so does your witness. How you react to little annoyances, how you manage your children and pets, how you leave a campsite when you move on—all these are witnesses for Christ.

You can look for ways to express God's love to others. You might ask your camping neighbors to join your evening campfires for singing and sharing. You may participate in a public worship service conducted on the grounds. Or you may find opportunity to speak with a neighbor about God's love in Christ. Witnessing is little problem for those who walk with the Lord.

The Christian who is silent about his faith back home is not likely to speak out when on vacation. If you have to program witnessing, something is wrong. When your life exhibits joy and freedom, you will never lack an audience for the Gospel.

5
Home-Based Adventure

Just what is outdoor adventure? Outdoor adventure includes activities that take place in a natural, outdoor setting, usually with nature-oriented objectives. These activities should be noncompetitive and require personal involvement.

For example, golf and tennis are great family sports, but are not within our definition of outdoor adventure. Downhill skiing, snowmobiling, trail bike riding, nights at the Y pool, competitive running, and many other active forms of recreation are excluded from this category because they require mechanical help or include competition. Our activities center in nature unimproved by asphalt, and in travel unaided by engines.

Our definition for outdoor adventure is admittedly narrow and arbitrary, and we claim no superior excellence for the simpler, nature-oriented activities we describe. But we do confess a bias against the snorting, smoking, engine-powered devices that delight so many. Their dust and the smell of exhaust seem out of place on a mountain trail. And if you've ever seen what a snowmobile does to a ski trail through the woods, you will know how we feel about that.

Our apologies to you who love your machines. Perhaps we're the poorer for sticking to foot and paddle power. One unforgettable March afternoon in the Wyoming Range taught us the utter delight of getting about, through impassible snows on a snow machine that carried us far beyond the range of skis. So we're gentle in our prejudice.

Backyard Adventure

Quite a while ago we learned that wilderness is a state of mind rather than a place. There's no difference between the stars over a city and the skies above the Alaska mountains. We should cultivate an appreciation for the outdoors throughout the year, not only on vacation trips. Responsible families should lead a balanced life, allowing selected days and hours for recreation. There's a lot of the outdoors you can enjoy in your backyard, and in the countryside within a short drive from home.

We moved to a home on the fringe of our city, a parsonage with a one-acre lawn! Mowing that lawn became an adventure when we noted 11 different wild flowers growing in the grass. It was painful to clip the blue violets on the moist lower corner, and to trim the wild strawberry blossoms that grew near the woods. Ten different kinds of trees grow in the yard of the new home we purchased, plus lilacs and other decorative shrubs. On the hills behind our home are scores of different kinds of trees and shrubs, many different kinds of flowers, 10 or more species of animals, and one of the nation's best known hawk flyways.

Miles of trails wind through the forested hills and valleys nearby, and a 200-mile trail is being developed along the ridge that follows the shore of Lake Superior.

Think of what you might find within a few miles of your home, or within a 100-mile radius of where you live. There's probably a lifetime of outdoor adventure within ready reach of your homes.

Almost every skill required for camping can be practiced in the backyard, and this creates a spirit of adventure for the family. Children can be taught how to build fires and cook outdoors. Mom and Dad might feel silly sleeping in a backyard tent, but the kids will love it. And a night or two of practice will make a first campout much more pleasant. Children bring a different set of values to the outdoors, and if an activity isn't fun, forget it.

Can you identify the trees that grow in your block? How many different kinds of birds do you suppose pause in your yard each year? What are their names? What constellations can you find? Can you point out the North Star to your son or daughter? There's a whole lot of outdoor discovery you can make without leaving your yard.

Things to Do Near Home

For some families the outdoors nearby will satisfy the need to relate to God's good world. Not everyone will take to the highways and wilderness trails. The fact that the family returns to its home to sleep does not rob children or parents of the values found in outdoor adventure. Dads whose work keeps them close to home, or away from home for extended periods will find greater value in backyard adventure.

1. On-land adventure. Jogging has captured the nation. Why not family jogging? To run on city sidewalks would not quite fit our definition, but jogging on a country lane would. As in every family activity, the pace and length of a run would have to be geared to the endurance of the children. Or maybe to Dad!

For those with a low level of enthusiasm for jogging, the old-fashioned hike will do. A brisk walk supplies most of the values of running, and might lead to that more sophisticated exercise.

Trails can be found in most county and state parks. If your home is within reach of larger wooded tracts, you will likely find many miles of trails set aside for hiking. A hike should generally have a predetermined purpose, some destination of special interest. Hiking blends well with other family interests, such as bird, tree, flower, or rock identification.

Some overnight hiking areas allow opportunity to sharpen backpacking skills for use later on more challenging treks.

Biking is another option for the family. We will look at the bike tour later in the book, but the all-day ride, or a pleasant few hours, can be enjoyed in every area.

Biking can begin with tot carriers on the parents' bikes, then graduate to bikes for each child as he grows. Many rides can begin at home and cover the neighborhood, but ultimately, the family will hook on a bike rack and take the family car to the countryside for more demanding pathways. Many communities have active cycle clubs that encourage the development of bikeways. Information about equipment and bike trails can be secured from cycle shops.

For occasional riding the bicycles need not be the more expensive 10-speed variety. Children's first bikes should be as simple as is practicable, for they will soon outgrow them. Bikes must be well maintained, and safe riding procedures taught and enforced.

Parents will probably wish to reserve some time for personal rides, allowing greater distances and speeds.

2. On-water adventure. Families living reasonably near lakes and rivers have a rich opportunity for adventure by canoe or kayak. The kayak tends to be more of a sporting craft than a means of quiet transportation across the waters, but with proper instruction and experience, families can enjoy exciting rides.

Power boats with their potential for pulling skiers provide another delightful form of family recreation, but this lies outside our definition for outdoor adventure. Yet who would deny the fun of a fishing trip in a boat driven by an outboard with Mom, Dad, and the kids aboard!

Sailing is another exciting water sport. With the increasing cost of fuel, wind power will find increasing favor among families that enjoy the water.

But why not a rowboat? Our speed-conscious society has surrendered almost entirely to engines to move its boats, but a fleet of rowboats hauling several families to an island picnic should not be scorned.

The canoe, however, seems to hold a special, romantic place in the hearts of outdoor-minded people. Our battered canoe makes up the total fleet at our house, and it has accounted for some of our most delightful adventures, some of which we will share in a later chapter.

Canoeing is completely safe when the craft is understood and proper instruction has been given. Life jackets should be worn whenever the family takes to the water. If this rule is observed, safety is practically assured. Remember that a person afraid of the water can drown even when wearing a life jacket if panic takes over.

The preventive for this is deliberate, simulated accidents. This involves loading the canoe for a typical trip, and then swamping it in reasonably shallow water. Passengers should be clothed as they would be on a trip. Nonswimmers should be able to feel the security a life jacket provides when they are suddenly cast into the water. Procedures for recovering the canoe and returning to land should be rehearsed.

When small children are included, the person responsible for each child should practice aiding the youngster, explaining in advance to the child what is about to happen, and giving him prior experience in shallow water. In this way, the child discovers the safe support of a life jacket.

Persons who refuse to wear flotation vests or life jackets should firmly be refused access to the canoes. Many tragedies could have been averted by insisting on this safety precaution. Under normal conditions a canoe is fully safe. But when canoes are improperly used, accidents can happen.

Family swims can complement almost any kind of outdoor activity that brings the family near a beach. Every parent and child should learn how to swim for the sheer delight of it, and for safety in other activities.

3. *Highways and byways.* About 100 miles from our home along the north shore of Lake Superior stands a stockade. Within it are the reconstructed reminders of our history, the days of the voyageurs. Guides take you through the old fort and tell the story of the North Country's first white canoeists. The tales of Indian ways are told as well.

Less than 100 miles in the other direction, the Connor Fur Trading Post awaits visitors. Authentically restored, this historic spot reminds you of the time when canoeing and hiking were not recreational forms, but part of life. To the north lies Itasca State Park with the headwaters of the Mississippi and a glorious stand of virgin white pine.

History surrounds our city, yet many families have never visited the sites. An amazing number of people confess they have never driven the 100 miles to the Boundary Waters Canoe Area, the world's most famous canoe country.

What does your area offer your family by way of outdoor discovery? It's a rare community that has not developed pioneer villages or historic centers which tell the story of the past when outdoor living was a necessity. Many interest centers include walking trails and picnic areas. Often, excellent bike routes can be discovered in the immediate vicinity.

Build a list of rewarding day trips your family can take. But start when the children are small. Kids who grow up on a TV diet soon lose interest in active living.

4. Collecting and identifying. Give your family a dinner-time quiz. Ask how many birds they can identify by name. How many trees and wildflowers? How many rocks or shells do they know?

One autumn day strange cars began arriving in our church parking lot. More and more arrived. The people walked quietly to one corner of the lot and peered up at a telephone pole. Obviously, they were observing something that was hidden from our view. Several dozen people were looking at an owl.

The owl obligingly perched on a spike of the pole for an hour or more, unperturbed by its audience. I discovered the owl was of a species rarely seen in that area. Alerted by phone, some of these people had traveled more than 100 miles on the chance that the owl would remain in the area. Others had responded to CB radio alerts. All this fuss over a little owl!

Bird-watching has become an enriching passion for many people. Why not acquaint your family with birds? The Audubon Society in your neighborhood will welcome you with enthusiasm and materials to help you bird-watch near your home.

Tree and shrub identification can become a delightful game as you hike through the woods. From spring through fall the woodlands and fields abound with wild flowers, far more than most people imagine. Beaches along the oceans are rich with shells. Inland beaches and gravel pits hide agates and other semiprecious stones. Nature offers many intriguing challenges: fossils, Indian arrowheads, bits of petrified wood. Might your family enjoy discovering more about some of these?

A valuable aid to nature study is the camera. When children learn that pictures can represent more than clusters of people or the baby's latest antic, photography takes on a new meaning. Outdoor photography preserves the adventures a family enjoys. It makes tangible the natural objects a family identifies but cannot collect and mount.

Moths and butterflies, along with other insects, make an interesting display with the name of each species neatly written below it. But how do you mount a bird? A photograph will give equal thrill when that picture was taken by a family member. Flowers should not be picked, for they fade immediately. But a close-up photograph will last for a long time.

The mysteries of photography frighten many families away from all but the simplest cameras. Yet with special care excellent photos can be made even with the simple Instamatics. The 35 mm camera with close-up and telephoto lenses opens the way to exciting adventures for the family. With basic instruction and practice, almost anyone can become a competent photographer, adding a lasting dimension to outdoor activities of all kinds. The new automatic single lens reflex cameras make photography available to anyone able to purchase one. Learning how to understand film speed, stops, depth of field, and shutter control is within the ability of anyone with the patience to read a bit and practice a lot.

Reliable instruction books for enjoying birds and trees, flowers, rocks, insects, stars and wildlife are discussed in the closing chapter.

5. *Hunting and fishing.* The shooting sports, including archery, have come under heavy attack in recent years, largely as a result of the nation's struggle with handgun control. When the risk to human life is removed from the debate, it appears clear that sport hunting is one means of controlling the population of certain game animals and birds. All sportsmen of character acknowledge that killing endangered species is wrong.

Only a pure vegetarian will attack hunting on the grounds that killing for food is immoral. Every beef steak and pork chop was once part of a living creature. If utilizing an animal for human need were wrong, then leather belts and shoes, purses and coats would have to be abolished.

Hunting has held a fascination for mankind throughout history, but killing for the sheer pleasure of shooting something seems to fulfill no noble purpose. The challenge of a true hunt, unaided by vehicles or aircraft, is a worthy adventure for families that hold this tradition.

As the world grows more crowded and more people turn to the outdoors for spiritual therapy, hunting raises another question. In those areas with limited wilderness, does the nonhunter have as much right to see live animals as the hunter has to see dead game? This is a question which wildlife authorities in each area will have to solve, based on space and game availability.

Family fishing can be practiced in most of the country with satisfying results. Fanatic fishing fathers must be reminded that children do not require trophy-size muskies to be satisfied. Panfish can be caught with ease in many regions. Larger fish can be sought on canoe trips, or trolled for on leisurely boat rides. Fishing can be one dimension of a day at the lake.

Along with learning how to catch and identify fish, youngsters should be taught how to dress and cook the catch. The mysteries of lures and other tackle will come in time. All fishermen should recognize that most fishing tackle is designed to hook fishermen, not fish. A small kit of carefully chosen lures will do about as well as the giant, tiered tackle boxes displayed on TV.

The joy and how-to of fishing could fill a book, and the friendly tackle merchant will offer more advice than a family can absorb. But a youngster who discovers the wonders of a lake or stream will possess a resource for a life of pleasure.

6. *Adventure for all seasons.* We who live in the North learn that outdoor adventure does not close in September when the beach does. Since winter or its close approximation extends for about six months, we enjoy cold weather sports also.

We have of late in the North discovered the cross-country ski and snowshoe. These historic implements for winter travel were outdazzled by downhill skiing, sometimes known as "yoyo skiing" by the ski touring buffs. Certainly, the ski slopes offer fascinating family recreation, but the ski touring possibilities should not be overlooked.

Many miles of groomed trails await the skier, with almost unlimited opportunity for snowshoe hiking when snow conditions are right. Sharing a winter weekend out-of-doors with several families promises much good for everyone.

Scattered throughout the snow country, you will find Christian camps that rent skis and snowshoes, and maintain excellent trails. Winter family weekends will become increasingly available as families find short trips more attractive.

Mark Your Calendar

We have identified 22 specific outdoor adventures for families to consider, and suggested several others on the fringe of our definition. No doubt you will think of other activities important to your family. What counts now is involvement. Mark your calendar!

Sharing the outdoors close to home has several obvious advantages. Since you return home to sleep, you need no mobile housing or motel money. Meals can be carried in a picnic basket. One free day is all you need, or even part of a day. The opportunity for sharing the outdoors with other families is unlimited.

Near-home adventure becomes a rehearsal for longer trips

and more challenging terrain. Skills can be mastered without fear that failure will bring disaster. Safe camping and waterfront attitudes can be established.

Exercise your mind and body. Get outdoors! Exercise your spirit too, and bring this vitality to the lives of your children in new and compelling ways. Play and laugh with them. Worship with them outdoors. Teach them to share with others.

Demonstrate the "whatsoever" gospel Paul wrote about when he said, "And whatsoever you do in word or deed, do all in the name of the Lord Jesus, giving thanks to God and the Father by Him" (Col. 3:17).

6
Resident Family Camping

An approach to outdoor adventure for the family that properly belongs in our discussion might be called Resident Family Camping. Here the family moves into a guest facility and participates in whatever activities the facility affords. For convenience we will consider two forms of resident camping: the lodge, ranch, or resort where the family puts together its own program, and the structured family camp where the family participates in a program planned by members of the camp staff.

The advantages of resident family camping are several. For one thing, there are no expenses for camping gear, shelter, campground fees and the inevitable emergencies that accompany life on the open road. Also, Mom is free from housework and Dad is free from looking after a camping rig, the car, and assorted bits of camping gear.

At first glance it may appear that resident family camping is more expensive since rental or registration fees come in one chunk. But very often this proves not to be the case when the total cost of a travel or wilderness camp is reviewed. Camping gear and travel trailers that sit around unused most of the year cost money, even when they're paid for.

Also, some families enjoy outdoor adventure but do not particularly like the rigors of camping out. They prefer to spend the time enjoying the program features available to them in a new area. Even veteran campers appreciate a change of pace now and then.

Do-It-Yourself Resident Camping

A wide variety of guest lodges, resorts, and rental cabins are available to families in almost every part of the country. Some provide all meals, some breakfast and supper. Accommodations may be modern or rustic. Usually, housekeeping units serve families that choose to prepare their own meals. Costs vary greatly according to the services offered. Readers of Christian periodicals will notice advertisements for guest ranches and lodges that cater to Christian families. The atmosphere of most facilities of this nature should be acceptable to Christian families, though prior investigation is essential in order to determine that offensive entertainment or program features are not present.

The guest ranch provides special delight for youngsters, with riding and the usual trappings of the West. With trail rides, wrangler breakfasts, cookouts, rodeos, campfire sings, the mood of the range is maintained. A cowboy hat seems almost necessary!

In the Midwest and East, guest farms invite guests for a few days or a week. Often these are working farms and family members have opportunity to share in doing the chores. Milk cows hold a fascination for children. The kids may be allowed to gather eggs, feed the pigs, dig potatoes, or whatever happens to be taking place at the time. Sometimes a mare will foal or a cow will calve, allowing children to share in this wonder.

The guest farm generally serves only two or three families at a time, giving the advantage of personal attention from the hosts. Pony rides and pony carts sometimes are offered. Of course, plain home cooking commands attention.

Amish families who serve guests provide a glimpse of the simple life. Their farms can be found in Ohio, Pennsylvania, and western New York.

Throughout the nation families will find guest lodges and resorts featuring the recreational opportunities of their region. Travel and camping magazines are filled with their ads. A visit to an outdoors and camping show in any major city will allow you to chat with lodge owners and collect brochures.

You can find slick operations with indoor pools, private golf courses, tennis courts and plush rooms. Or you can find rustic resorts with Spartan cabins and outdoor privies. The fee will reflect the difference.

Timber Wolf Point resort near Buyck, Minnesota offers families a genuine wilderness experience without the need for camping out. Located within the Superior National Forest, guests can reach the Boundary Waters Canoe area by a short paddle and a portage. Operated by a Christian family, the small resort maintains hiking trails, a fleet of boats and canoes, a small store with bait and fishing tackle, and a family picnic area on Timber Wolf Point. Deer, moose, and bears are sometimes seen at the resort. A rustic atmosphere is deliberately maintained to give the feel of the genuine wilderness which surrounds the resort.

Another approach to family resident camping is offered at Runnings Retreat on Comstock Lakes just north of Duluth, Minnesota. The Runnings family keeps the lawns neatly trimmed. A pontoon boat roams the three connecting lakes in search of fish. A few chickens and geese share the lawns with campers. The beach and dock provide safe swimming. The cabins are simple and tourist interests in the surrounding area are featured.

Near Grand Marais along the north shore of Lake Superior is Cascade Lodge, another facility operated by Christian people. The restaurant is superb; the housing facilities range from housekeeping cabins to top quality rooms in the lodge. There are hiking trails along the Cascade River and Lake Superior. During summer months a program staff is available to guests, and excellent skiing, both downhill and cross-country, attracts winter visitors.

Guest facilities like these provide a happy retreat for vacationing families, allowing them to enjoy all the outdoor adventure they wish without the demands of setting up camp.

The disadvantage lies in the lack of privacy a family enjoys in its own camp, and in occasional intrusions by people who tend to spoil the quiet atmosphere. But initiative on the part of parents can overcome these minor problems.

Programmed Resident Family Camping

The first family camp on record was a Christian camp, the frontier camp meeting. Families camped out because there was no other way! Lacking large meeting halls, outdoor gatherings were necessary. Modern Christian resident camping traces its roots to these frontier camp meetings.

Twenty years ago the great Bible conferences seemed doomed. Aging facilities and small crowds appeared to mark the end of an era. Then family camping revived. Today Bible conferences and Christian camps thrive on family weeks which often attract capacity crowds. Programs have changed considerably, however, from the pattern established for many years in the old Bible conference centers.

In contrast with the resort or lodge center for family adventure, the Bible conference provides a complete program for every family member. It might be questioned whether this kind of experience properly belongs within our definition for outdoor adventure. But take a look at what is happening in family camp!

Breakfast may be served from 7:30 to 9:00, allowing families to come when they wish. Rather than a full schedule of meetings, most of the day is reserved for family-centered activity. The program staff is available to serve as needed. Organized activities are presented as an option, and families are encouraged to choose from the many offered.

Morning and evening gatherings feature programs that appeal to the entire family. Certain hours may be set aside for adult instruction and fellowship, with staff people leading graded activity for children, and with sitters available for the little ones.

The resident family camp compromises family togetherness somewhat, but the compromise is deliberate, blending family times with special interest meetings. Teens come to know other teens. Children share together. Husbands and wives enjoy relaxed times in fellowship with other parents. Meals are times for getting acquainted.

Family projects are encouraged. One camp holds a sand castle competition that requires every family member to participate. Family skits are presented. While quite different than a wilderness trip, the family camp accomplishes much good for the home.

Families are housed together, of course. Early attempts at family camping found some camps utilizing the cabins as they would for youth camps, men in one section and women in another. A few programmed much like they did for junior camp, with every minute of the day filled. Such camps failed. Now cabins are divided so each family has private quarters. Camps have developed tent and trailer sites to accommodate more families. And the daily schedule is relaxed, with much time for the family to explore the outdoors and enjoy program facilities offered by the camp.

The Caravan Camp

Since the next two chapters will be concerned primarily with individual families camping alone, or with one or two other families in a nonstructured manner, we will take a look at one additional form of resident family camping: the caravan camp.

In this form of camping, each family provides its own housing, either a recreation vehicle or a tent. A group of families gathers in a private or public camping area to share a weekend or week together. Usually, a loosely structured program is planned.

The advantages of this kind of camping lie in its versatility and economy. The location can move from year to year, and since each family prepares its own meals, the expense to the family is minimized.

We have shared in several caravans of this nature and found caravaning to be a delightful approach to outdoor adventure. That Memorial Day weekend campout referred to previously was particularly rewarding. Families of all ages and economic brackets shared the campsite. God did a good work in many hearts.

The retreat took place in a public camping area near a small river in Nebraska. Providentially, a Christian farm family lived adjacent to the camp. They offered a burro for the children to ride, and wagon rides to several historic sites. The river offered fishing, though I don't recall that any fish were caught.

The large center area of the camp was alive with impromptu softball and volleyball games. No recreation program was planned, and though more than 100 people participated, no tensions developed during the 4 days.

Two all-camp activities were planned for each day: a morning and late afternoon campfire. The programs included lively singing and a story message. Brief and pointed, the programs focused on the positive joys of knowing Christ.

The late evening hours were deliberately left open for family campfires. How delightful it was to stand in the center of the camping area and see a dozen or more small fires flickering in the darkness! Some families brought lanterns. Families invited neighbors to share their fires and snacks. The songs from many campfires blended together. A group of teenagers gathered around one fire, singing to the strumming of a guitar.

Some talked, laughed, and sang far into the night. No one rang a bell. One by one the fires burned low and silence fell over the circle of camping families. The next day would be filled with families driving off to explore the area, or hiking along the river, or traveling to the dam to fish. The family caravan is a worthy expression of outdoor adventure.

Making New Friends
In the early chapters we discussed the importance of building spiritual strength through choosing the right friends. We said that friendship cannot be commanded, and that a mutually enjoyable environment is essential for youth friendships to prosper.

Camping with other Christian families encourages such friendships to develop. These are times parents should covet as they help their children through the difficult years of adolescence. While times alone with the family are vital, times spent with other families are important too. One experience common to almost all parents, and shocking to each in his turn, is the phenomenon of sudden indifference exhibited by young teenagers concerning sharing trips with parents. Teens much prefer being with their peers. When a camping trip includes other teenagers, this indifference generally disappears!

The change in feelings toward family that steals over teens is not a sign of rebellion, nor a lack of love. It is simply social development taking over. When this occurs in your family, try camping with other families that have teenage young people. Or invite guests who are about the age of your children. Friendships are vitally important to your children during the teenage years.

7
The Open Road

Two kinds of family camping remain to be explored: the travel camp along the highways and back roads, and the wilderness trip. First, let's consider the travel camp.

The fuel crisis of the late 70s lowered the boom on unrestricted travel camping, sending the recreation vehicle industry scurrying to the drawing boards to find alternatives to their gas-gobbling land yachts. The industry will succeed, for there's no evidence that people intend to quit camping. At this writing several firms have designed mini-motorhomes fully self-contained, yet fitting on the chassis of subcompact pickups. These mini-motorhomes boast better than 15 miles per gallon on the highways. This is in contrast with 5 miles per gallon for the big motorhomes.

But families can find other alternatives for camping. Compact trailers, rigs that can be towed behind any family car, have served European campers for years. The low-profile tent camper, light enough to haul without special hitches even by a compact family car, will gain popularity. And there is nothing wrong with a tent. One benefit brought about by the energy crunch is the discovery that we need not take all the comforts of home into the campground.

Read travel camping magazines and attend camping and outdoor shows to keep abreast of industry developments in camping rigs. Fight the temptation to buy one of the big rigs that will flood the market at bargain prices. The person selling it has a mighty good reason! When you buy, buy quality, for a travel rig will last many years if it is sound to begin with and given proper maintenance.

A caution sounded elsewhere bears repeating here. Unless you plan to camp often, it may be better to rent rather than buy. When you figure up the initial cost plus finance charges, insurance, depreciation, maintenance, license, and possibly storage fees, you may find the cost per day prohibitive. Remember too that hauling any rig cuts your mileage significantly.

But why not buy a tent? Our ease-loving society scorns the thought of sleeping under canvas, but many have never tried it. A good tent properly pitched, when supplied with adequate provision for sleeping, can be fully satisfying. Rain complicates tenting, though you can sleep dry in a downpour if the tent has been chosen carefully. Packing a wet tent calls for a philosophical outlook.

Tent heaters function well and safely. Cots are compact and comfortable as we shall learn later. A tent fly keeps you shaded and dry when cooking outdoors. Tents do not provide showers and hot running water, nor do they afford suitable plumbing, but a corner screened off can conceal any one of several patented devices that substitute satisfactorily for the missing toilet. Bugs are no more of a problem in a properly screened tent than in a recreation vehicle with traffic moving in and out the door.

Best of all, you can buy excellent tents for a small fraction of the cost of the cheaper RVs, and the tents will last for many years when carefully handled.

Tents exist in so many styles and price ranges we will not attempt to discuss them fully here. Avoid the ultra lightweight nylon fabrics for family use, however. They sweat miserably as the temperatures drop at night, leaving the interior clammy, and a fine mist falls each time a breeze shakes the frame. A fine count cotton fabric serves well, and can be waterproofed.

Here are two cautions, in case you miss them in your study of tents. Never spray insect repellent directly on the tent. It will destroy the waterproofing of cotton cloths, and sometimes eat holes in synthetic fabrics. Second, when it is raining, do not press anything against the tent from inside. The tent will leak at that point and continue to leak until the cloth has a chance to dry. Watch especially that children sleeping on pads on the floor do not roll against the side of the tent during a rain. Their sleeping bags will soon be soaked.

Two safety precautions should be taken. Never use open flames in a tent. Candles are dangerous, for some tents are highly flammable, and even fire-retardant tents will burn. Nylon tents will quickly melt from sparks or flame. When you camp in country inhabited by bears, never keep food or cosmetics in the tent. Bears have a strange affinity for your groceries, even toothpaste. More will be said about animal dangers in the next chapter.

How you store a tent is very important. Never pack a tent when wet. If you are traveling and rain falls, roll the tent loosely and pack it on top of your load so you can lay it out to dry at the first opportunity. A tent will grow musty and will mildew within a few hours if packed away wet.

There's something about a family sharing a tent that breaks down artificial emotional barriers. And a tent makes possible the joys of camping for families with limited incomes.

Family Camping Equipment

Having looked at the choices in travel and shelter for the family as they camp, the next consideration is basic equipment needs for comfortable outdoor living. The variety and price range are so vast that you must study your needs carefully. Talk with experienced campers and visit camping shops. Buy good quality, even though you may not plan to camp extensively. Cheap becomes costly when you are using camping gear.

Obviously, your choice of gear will differ according to the type of camping you plan. Backpacking demands minimum gear; the canoe trip with short portages allows slightly more; the pack animal trip more yet; and auto camping tempts the family to empty the house.

As you gain experience, you will discover how simple life can become; and you will learn how dependent we are on frills and gadgets! Impulse packing inevitably clutters a trip, often causing some essentials to be forgotten. Carefully planned, the disciplined selection of personal and camping gear brightens your camping day before it begins.

A Good Night's Sleep

Two of the most important dimensions of family camping are eating and sleeping. Without satisfying meals and ample rest, nothing else will count for much. Camping vehicles can accommodate the sheets and blankets from home, but this only complicates camp life. The sleeping bag offers the most practical answer to the bedding problem. The fiber-filled bag serves best in the moderate price line. The bag should contain at least three pounds of filler, unless you camp in a hot climate. Warmer bags are not ordinarily needed for the typical family camp, and a spare blanket is a happier solution than a bulky sleeping bag that proves too warm for most nights.

If you plan frequent pack trips, the down-filled bags may be worth the added cost. Again, choose a bag that suits your average need. Should you wish to camp in colder weather, carry a down liner or buy down-filled underwear for pajamas.

The best pajamas are a pair of loose-fitting cotton pants and an equally loose-fitting hooded sweat shirt. In extremely mild weather, the sweat shirt may be replaced with a T-shirt. With this attire, getting up is less traumatic on a cool morning. You are already respectably dressed, and you can tend to early morning chores by adding only moccasins or sneakers. When the camp is under control, you can change to your regular clothes.

The hooded sweat shirt is important because the head accounts for much of the heat loss that makes for cold sleeping. Another warming trick calls for a pair of wool socks reserved for sleeping. Never go to bed wearing damp socks. Tuck them into the sleeping bag, and they will be dry in the morning.

When you are camping by auto, you probably will find sufficient space to haul camp cots, at least for the adults. Camp cots are worth the space and effort. Put foam pads on the cots and sleep as comfortably as you do at home. If you have pitched your tent on a fairly level spot, free from rocks, foam pads on the ground will do for the children.

To keep dampness from the floor, lay a plastic sheet under the tent floor. Be sure this does not extend beyond the perimeter of the tent, for rain will run down the tent sides and collect on top of the plastic, soaking the floor instantly. Some argue against plastic if the tent is to be left standing for a considerable time. A good trick for any tent that remains in one spot for several days is to occasionally place several sticks under the floor to allow air to circulate, making the tent more pleasant.

Air mattresses are losing favor to foam pads. Pads never go flat in the middle of the night and they do not require inflation.

They weigh less than air mattresses, even though they appear more bulky. An inch-and-a-half of foam gives more effective insulation than an air mattress. If you do use an air mattress, be certain that it contains only enough air to keep you off the ground. When you sit up, you should feel the ground. Cots with foam pads insure good sleeping. On the trail, just carry the pad. If you want pillows, and have room, take them along.

The question of heating tents and trailers must be considered with extreme care. A properly designed furnace takes care of tent trailers and mobile homes. Several firms manufacture catalytic heaters using white gas, or propane-fueled heaters. They are efficient, but adequate ventilation *must* be provided. While these heaters are relatively fumeless, they burn sizable quantities of oxygen. Never use charcoal for heating or cooking inside. Charcoal gives off deadly carbon monoxide. All heating systems should be inspected regularly to assure safe operation.

Camp Cooking

Camp cooking differs little from home cooking. You can cook almost anything in camp you would serve at home, if you bring along the right gear. Not many campers attempt fancy baking, though this is possible too.

The source of heat must be decided upon. Open fires are romantic, but a nuisance for cooking, and they are being banned more and more by public and private camps. In some areas firewood is unavailable. Charcoal is a viable option, but it is messy and slow unless you invest in a patented charcoal-starting rig. The best solution for day-to-day auto camp cooking seems to be the LP gas stove.

Those who camp with recreation vehicles usually have a built-in stove. Others can buy a two- or three-burner model for a reasonable price. The trend seems to be away from the pressure gasoline models, even though they provide excellent heat if handled properly. Serious accidents have resulted from carelessness or ignorance. White gas is treacherously volatile.

The most economical method is the LP gas stove with a refillable gas supply. The small, throwaway cylinders serve well, but they increase the cost and they always seem to run out in mid-oatmeal. When camping in the mountains, expect a decrease in the heat output of your LP stove.

Recreation vehicle owners soon build an efficient collection of cooking gear, but tent campers must work at it. A plywood camp box designed to hold your cooking equipment will prove valuable. You can buy precut models to assemble at home, or you can design your own. An assortment of cardboard boxes is less than satisfactory.

Nesting camp cook kits serve well, though you will need a supplementary griddle or fry pan. When you cook over charcoal or an open fire, be sure to soap the exterior of every pot. You will find the soot rinses off easily when cooking chores are done.

Many camping parks provide a picnic table at each site, and tent campers have tables inside. But tenters may want to purchase a light folding table and camp stools. A couple of folding lawn chairs feel great at day's end, especially when you plan to spend several days in one spot.

While the traveling camper may want to plan menus in advance, food may be purchased along the way rather than hauling groceries from home. Although ice for the cooler is available in most places, it is more practical to purchase milk and meats each day.

Some Miscellaneous Advice

Here are bits of knowledge that will contribute to your comfort and peace of mind while traveling:

1. Use traveler's checks and oil company credit cards.

2. Leave a copy of your itinerary with family or close friends.

3. In season state parks in populous areas are usually filled up by Friday at noon. Private campgrounds will be less crowded for your Friday and Saturday overnights.

4. National park campgrounds fill up every day in season, so schedule your arrival before midafternoon.

5. National forest campsites in the sparsely populated areas of the West are usually not crowded. If near the highway, they may fill up late in the evening, but there is usually room for more. These campsites are generally free and represent the ideal kind of camping we dream about. Dry toilets and no washrooms are the rule.

6. If your car is heavily loaded in hot weather, use brakes sparingly, carry extra water, and try to schedule the bad mountain grades for the cool of the morning.

7. Do not carry large supplies of food. Shop daily and only stock up when you are going to stay several days in a national park or forest where you cannot be sure of finding good stores.

8. High altitudes can get very cold at night in midsummer. Carry medium or lightweight sleeping bags plus one sheet and one blanket per bed. In cold weather, sleeping on the ground is much warmer than on a cot without a pad.

9. Use layers of clothing. Sport shirts, cotton slacks, one sweater, and one medium or heavyweight jacket will provide flexibility and warmth. Use wash-and-wear clothing to minimize ironing.

10. Heavy-duty cartons are ideal for clothing and food boxes. Cartons stack easily and are handier than suitcases and large chuck boxes.

11. A propane lantern and stove is safer than the gasoline model.

12. A small hand ax and a 20-inch tow-type saw are all you need for cutting firewood. Keep the ax sharp and sheathed! Use it only for splitting or trimming.

13. Insect repellent is a must. Use it at the first sign of mosquitoes or chiggers. If in grassy areas, put repellent on ankles, socks, and pant cuffs. The cream repellents are the most economical and easiest to apply. Sticks and sprays are more expensive and harder to apply. Carry a bug bomb for your tent when necessary, but don't spray the canvas!

Sandy or beach areas may have armies of ants. Chlorinated cleanser sprinkled on the ground will turn back ants. If your camping outfit is not insect tight, also use the cleanser at points of access such as trailer legs.

14. When in very hot weather, keep camera film under clothing or blankets to avoid high temperatures.

15. Watch your camera exposures in the West. Long-range mountain scenes require 1/2 stop less than normal. Desert scenes require about a full stop less. If normal is f 8 at 1/100, use f 11. A haze filter is a good investment for open shade and marine or mountain scenes. Consult your camera store for other tips on photography.

16. Aluminum cups are not good for drinking hot liquids. Use them for soups or salads and get some plastic cups for coffee.

17. Pack your top carrier as though wrapping a package, by laying an eight-by-ten-foot tarp on the bottom and folding it in from both sides, then back to front and front to back. Use web straps. Mount carrier as far forward as possible to balance car load. There is an unexpected bonus in using a top carrier. It shades and insulates the car roof from the sun. With air space underneath, the carrier can keep the car as much as ten degrees cooler on a hot day.

18. If you intend to camp frequently in cool weather, a

catalytic heater is a good investment. However, remember to provide good ventilation for a heater, or any other heating or cooking equipment in a closed area.

The Joys of the Road

Camping along the highways opens the way for a wide variety of family discoveries. Too often we make getting someplace the goal and pass by much that the family would enjoy.

On one of our trips, we drove through the Dakotas and Montana. We came to an area famed for its prairie dog villages. I pulled off the road so the children could see the quaint critters. Of course, everyone wanted to get out of the car for a closer look. But we worried about reaching our destination, so we hurried on. Unfortunately, our destination offered nothing to equal the appeal of a prairie dog village. We wish now that we had stopped for a few minutes longer.

Travel camping always holds the possibility of meeting the unexpected. Driving home from Alaska, we had an experience we have laughed about many times.

The sun was nowhere near cresting the hills when Elsie's urgent whisper awakened me. "Get up," she ordered. "I think there's a bear down the road." It takes a mighty exciting bear to stir my adrenaline before sunrise, even in the Yukon, but then I heard the cover of a garbage can clatter to the ground. I woke up. Elsie was tiptoeing, camera in hand, toward the sound as I slipped into my pants and moccasins. I caught up and we moved down the winding wooded road, expecting to observe a scavenger black bear at work.

Instead, we saw a tired-looking, swaybacked, black horse. He sniffed the scattered debris at his feet. Then, lifting his head, he spotted us and ambled our way, looking pleased to find someone up so early. The horse paused in front of us, obviously expecting some toll for our trespass.

We invited him to come along to our camp, which he did. I fed him bolten biscuits while Elsie snapped a picture in the dim light. The picture did not come out so well, but we laugh each time we see it. We remember a friendly, stray, black horse shuffling from camp to camp as though he were the official garbage inspector. That was a good day.

Just as you pace a trail trip according to the strength of your weakest camper, so you should plan your travel trip for the pleasure of your youngest family member. Camping must be fun, or else why go? Beware of long stops that hold interest only for adults. Provide pleasant diversion for the children too, or the value of the vacation will be lost.

Some families have taken serendipity trips. Choosing a direction, they did whatever their whim and budget allowed. They planned no schedule so they could never be late. Many family adventures have been ruined by hurry.

Travel guides abound in every state and province. Changes have come in travel accommodations, with many private camps adding tent sites to care for the increasing numbers of families who have adopted this kind of shelter.

Resist the temptation to pull off at some secluded spot to save a camping fee. Great personal danger for unprotected campers exists along the roads. Plan to stop by midafternoon to find a satisfactory campsite and to allow the children to play.

Campsites are available in national forests and parks, sometimes with a modest fee and/or a seasonal permit. These campsites frequently lack the amenities you find in a private campground.

The Joys off the Road
Travel campers should remember that outdoor adventure means leaving the asphalt or concrete to discover the world of nature. Take side hikes. Pause at a lake to swim or fish. Shoot

some pictures away from the roads. Check your travel guide for points of interest in the back country. Leave the freeways and drive the side roads. Don't hesitate to change your trip plan if you discover an unexpected point of interest.

The spiritual values of family adventure grow out of the total experience. When hassles develop on the highway, it's difficult to share an enjoyable campfire at night. Set your pace by the needs of the children. Remember that the purpose of a vacation trip is not to get somewhere, but to enjoy the going. Dad's and Mom's moods will determine how much fun the kids have. Plan frequently to leave the car and walk a bit. Most of the pleasure of a vacation trip lies off the road.

Where to Go?

As the dollar shrinks and travel costs swell, the family will plan more carefully where they go. The Christian family, especially, will want to make every trip count. Why not plan a trip that will include a visit to missionaries? Perhaps your family could spend a week helping a struggling mission church, or providing a ministry to a special people.

Stop by a church on Sunday morning and encourage a congregation. We remember how refreshing it was, when we served small country churches, to have Christian friends drop in.

Give your family all the exposure you can to the good world of nature. There's more to see and more hills to climb and more rivers and lakes to explore than any family could cover in 10 lifetimes. And as you travel remember your purpose: to rediscover your family outdoors.

8
Along the Wilderness Trail

We have considered outdoor adventure for families in several dimensions, offering opportunity for almost every preference in recreation. We turn now to the more dramatic and in some ways the most demanding kind of outdoor activity, the wilderness trip.

The wilderness trail is not for every family. However, for me, the canoe waters or high mountain trails hold a special fascination.

I would encourage every family to explore wilderness camping to taste the unique experiences to be found. Here is a world that places demands which are largely forgotten in our technological society. We find ourselves relating in a primary manner to the basics of survival.

The value of wilderness camping lies not only in the pleasure of new challenges, but in the potential such trips offer for enriching our children. I am profoundly grateful for the blend of influences that gave me a deep love for the outdoors. I would be much poorer without this love. No other activity I know about teaches initiative and self-reliance so effectively. We'll look at wilderness camping for the family, for fathers and sons, and for husbands and wives. I will begin with the men in the family, for I have seen what camping has done for my boys.

A Boy and a Mountain

I saw my son hike off one day with his sleeping bag tied to his pack. He headed up a high Alaskan mountain with meager rations in his pockets and a camera around his neck. He grinned and waved and said he would be back soon. A friend standing nearby said, "How can you let him go off alone like that? What if something happens?" I watched the boy disappear up the wooded trail and prayed that something indeed might happen. He was about 18 at the time.

Camping is good because it leads to self-discovery, and young people need to discover themselves. I knew this boy well, for we had camped together. I knew he possessed skills beyond mine and had agility I had long since lost. I knew too that dangers existed, but the risks were far less in those mountains than those he faced as he walked to school. When Dave hiked up the mountain I had not the slightest fear. I prayed something might happen, for you can hear very well on a mountain when it is still. Remember Elijah?

Building Dreams

So often I see myself in my sons, and I think about the way men grow. Not too long ago I slipped away to visit the haunts of my boyhood. I wanted to see how the woods and hills looked from an adult perspective, for I remembered much about my dreams as a boy. The hills seemed lower and the distances much shorter, but the little creek still flowed, and I suppose it grows to a torrent in the spring, just as it used to.

I hunted out the place where the first wild flowers bloomed each year, the blue and yellow violets, the May flowers and trilliums, the marsh marigolds—cowslips, we called them—and the wild roses. My secret wild plum tree was gone, dead of old age, I presumed. Both my tadpole pond and the spring, halfway up the hill, had dried up.

But my memories were fresh and flowing. What amazed me, as I thought back, was the number of dreams from 40 years ago and more that had been fulfilled. Without conscious plotting they had come to pass. I now believe that one of our biggest jobs as parents is to sow the right dreams in our children.

Long before I dared admit it, I wanted to be a preacher. There were days when I sat on the south side of the hill overlooking the lake and dreamed of writing stories and books. I longed to visit Alaska and prowl the mountains with my rifle in search of game. I wanted to own a fly rod and lure trout from the mountain streams.

These were not very sophisticated dreams. But each of them was fulfilled. But who planted those dreams? My parents had a part, of course, and the men who led our scout troop, and the boys whose company I sought. I felt again the obligation I owed those people, and I renewed my commitment to God to do what I could to help other boys dream. Family camping will build dreams for your sons and daughters, and the best dreams are found along the wilderness trail.

Dads and Sons on the Trail

I know a man who took each of his sons on a week-long canoe trip, when each boy reached the age of 12. The trip with his youngest son was unusually brief because a bear stole their food packs. But the trip that the youngster had looked forward to for six years had become a reality, and that was what mattered most.

Often, several fathers and sons will share a camping adventure. We have organized several trips of this nature, and would recommend that you give thought to this. One summer nine pairs of dads and sons from our home church took a canoe trip. Now the younger boys' eyes sparkle as they anticipate their turn.

Perhaps one of the finest father-son trips I have shared took place in the Cascades in northern Washington. The party totaled 30, including my two youngest sons. We combined backpacking and a horse pack experience; half the party hiked in and the other half rode, bringing a string of pack mules which carried most of our gear.

We enjoyed perfect weather. Scores of brook trout took to our lures. We also explored an old mine. Warm days yielded to the evening chill, making our campfires doubly appreciated.

The week passed swiftly, and near the end, a lad suffered an accident. Though painful, his injury permitted him to remain with the camp. His father tenderly looked after him. The lad's testimony at our closing campfire spoke to every father. He said, "I couldn't sleep much last night. But I did a lot of thinking. I straightened out some things with the Lord. And one more thing. Until last night, I wasn't really sure my dad cared for me. But now I know."

I wondered how well I had communicated love to my boys as they struggled with adolescence. The closeness camping requires might tell many boys that their dad really loves them.

Husband and Wife Out Camping

Trail camping is a rewarding adventure for husband and wife, either alone or with other couples. Though the trip must be paced to the needs of whichever partner is least secure, a few well-planned days on the trail can enhance any marriage.

Several years ago we shared a canoe trip with our pastor and his wife and one other couple. I confess the men engineered the time and place to coincide with the peak of spring trout fishing in Ontario. We drove to Minnesota, picked up our gear at Duane's Outfitters, and pushed off from Moose Lake heading for Canada. Progress was aided by a light outboard on a square stern which towed the other two canoes, a procedure which was legal then.

Warm sun and favorable winds made the first day delightful, but rain started falling as we pitched camp. The rain continued through the next day, making a three-quarter-mile portage more taxing than we cared for. But finally, we reached our base camp on That Man Lake and pitched the tents. The sky grew darker and a stiff wind blew in off the lake. The temperature dropped into the low 40s.

That was the story for the next two days. We slipped away between squalls and caught a few walleyes, but the trout eluded us. Most of the time was given to keeping the fire burning, preparing meals and cheering up one another. The women huddled under ponchos, glad for the foresight that included packing insulated underwear! Our three small tents flapped in the wind.

The third night the rain stopped and snow fell! When we crawled out of our tents in the morning, the sky had cleared and the landscape was breathtaking. Each tree and rock was frosted with fresh snow that glistened in the sun. The snow retreated before the rising sun and we took to the lake in search of trout.

How often over our late evening coffee we have remembered that trip! The adverse weather and cold have been forgotten. The mark of a camper is his ability to keep comfortable regardless of wind and weather, and to remain cheerful at the same time. We felt we had passed our test with good marks.

Camping as husband and wife in the sunshine is fun, and even adversity has a peculiar kind of pleasure. There is something good about being together in a world of beauty.

The Whole Family

Camping along the wilderness trail with the entire family challenges a growing number of people each year. A mistake some families make is to launch into too ambitious a venture without adequate preparation. There is no use pretending that difficulties do not exist. But this is the challenge of camping.

Do not wait too long to introduce children to trail camping. Begin with a day-long horseback ride or hike or canoe trip. Then graduate to an easy overnight where basic skills can be practiced. Gradually, take extended trips on more demanding trails. Many young people who reject wilderness camping were improperly introduced to trail life, or maybe the introduction came too late.

How early should camping adventure begin? Two of our grandchildren enjoyed their first trip when they were four. We spent three days on an island in the canoe country. The party spanned four generations, from my father who was 72, to his great-grandchildren. In between were our sons and a son-in-law. The little boys were fitted with small packs and miniature paddles.

The rule in all camping is to pace the program to the abilities of the weakest. When sufficient leadership is available, you can divide the group, providing more challenging activity for advanced campers; it is cruel to force a youngster beyond his abilities.

Provide a happy experience for your children and they will look forward year by year to trips with Mom and Dad. If you are a novice, team up with an experienced camping family for a fellowship trip.

Explore the delights of trail camping through day-long hikes and overnights from your auto camp. Many private and public camps offer nature trails and hikes to points of interest. Perhaps you could find a hiking trail near your home with picnic facilities or campsites for your use. You might even consider a backyard camp-out where you can figure out how that tent goes up!

Paddle, Saddle, and Afoot

Having considered some of the values and options for wilderness adventure, let's look at the practical matters involved. Space forbids a detailed discussion of any one kind of wilderness travel. I will provide an overview and refer you to resources that supply greater detail. Remember that wilderness camping becomes very personalized as to procedures and gear. For example, I dislike ponchos and despise air mattresses, while others live quite comfortably with both. Digging fire holes for cooking seems utterly foolish to me, but you still see pictures of them in camping books.

Opportunities for wilderness family camping take three basic forms: canoeing, horseback trips, and backpacking. Each possesses distinctive charms, but backpacking offers wide appeal since hiking trails can be found in most sections of the country. The remote horseback trip is largely confined to the western mountains, and real wilderness canoeing will be found in more limited areas than hiking trails, though satisfying river and lake trips are more widely available than most of us realize.

But whether walking, riding or paddling, you will discover muscles you had forgotten! Physical preparation is the first practical point to consider when you plan a wilderness trip. The kids will have far less problem with this than Mom and Dad.

Horseback Trip

For sheer romance it's hard to beat a saddle trip through the mountains. Those with a love for horses can ride for days and find each moment fulfilling. The creak of leather and the sight of a pack train following the riders brings back visions of pioneer days in the Old West.

However, pack trips are pretty much confined to the West, though rewarding trail rides are offered throughout the country. Since I'm not particularly fond of horses, I find a ride along traveled roads unexciting. Our trips through the Bridger National Forest of Wyoming and the High Cascades in Washington were outstanding.

Horse pack trips are the most expensive kind of wilderness travel, since horses eat all year long but work only a few weeks for their owners. Also, an experienced hand is needed for every five or six animals, and since one pack animal is required for each two or three riders, the guide cost runs high.

Yet I recall with pleasure that caravan of riders and pack horses that rode into the campsite by Dagger Lake in the Cascades as we were winding up a delightful day of fishing with our father-son group. We watched the smooth transition from trail to camp as the obviously experienced families moved in. Horses were unsaddled and rubbed down. Then some of them did their own rubbing down by rolling in the dust. Loads from pack horses combined into an efficient camp kitchen and a cluster of tents. Three families totaling perhaps 15 people enjoyed an evening meal which included freshly caught trout, a gift from a camp near the trail. We visited our neighbors and marveled at their competence in the outdoors. They would ride more than 100 miles through the mountains.

Riding was to them what walking is to most of us, so they found no unusual problems in a trail ride. However, we had to depend on professional packers at considerable cost.

Probably a ranch vacation is the most practical way for families to experience trail riding, spending some days with the horses, and other days in one of the many activities offered by guest ranches. Many Christian camps include horses in their programs for families, and guest ranches can be found that cater to Christian families especially.

Trail camping with horses presents the same kind of camping challenges found in backpacking and canoeing, except for the more generous provision of food and equipment made possible by pack horses or mules. For a delightful, whimsical look at this kind of camping, read *Horses, Hitches, and Rocky Trails,* by Joe Back, Swallow Press, Chicago. Even if you never go camping with horses, you'll enjoy this account by a professional packer and artist.

A letter to Christian Camping International, Box 400, Somonauk, Ill. 60552 will provide the names of Christian camps that offer horseback riding for families.

Canoe Camping

Since the basic camping experience is quite similar in all forms of wilderness travel, we will discuss briefly the general principles involved in canoeing and backpacking, spending a bit more time with backpacking. Later in the chapter we will review the provisions a family must consider when planning a wilderness trip.

Several areas in the U.S. and Canada offer excellent canoe routes for families. The canoe permits you to be less fussy about the weight of gear and food, but care is still required, for most routes include at least one portage.

Portaging a canoe is not difficult. The yoke balances the craft comfortably on your shoulders, though by the first evening you will be glad the portaging is over for that day. A 17-foot aluminum canoe weighs about 75 pounds, less for the lightweights, more for some models. Fiberglass canoes of similar dimensions weigh about the same with most features equaling the aluminum variety.

You must stay away from white water until you are

experienced, and you should *never* run rapids where the slightest doubt of safety exists. Canoeing is safe and enjoyable if you observe the rules.

We came upon an unforgettable scene one summer. A young man stood waist deep in swirling rapids trying to dislodge his overturned canoe from between two boulders. His gear had floated down the stream, and some had sunk irretrievably to the bottom. The small outboard motor had been his undoing. Approaching the landing above the rapids, he had cut the engine, but before he could retrieve his paddle from beneath the packs, the current had swept him into the rapids.

The canoe had overturned, spilling his wife and poodle into the froth. Fortunately, the stream was not deep and danger to life was small, but the drenched dog howled from a rock in midstream, and the wife howled from shore. I never heard a man take such a scolding! I suspect the remainder of the trip was quite uncomfortable.

In most canoe areas you will find outfitters eager to rent you canoes and other gear, eliminating the need for personal investment as you sample the joys of canoe camping.

Hiking

The simplest, and in many ways most rewarding, means of wilderness travel is hiking. Thousands of miles of marked trails await the traveler. The Appalachian Trail winds from Maine to Georgia, 2,050 miles along the ridges of the East. The Pacific Crest Trail covers 2,000 miles along western mountains. In between you can find all types of hiking terrain with all degrees of challenge.

As you might suspect, comfortable feet are the hiker's best friends. One blister can destroy an otherwise sound man on the trail. Choose your footgear well, and break them in thoroughly before starting your hike. Again, the art of backpacking involves too much for detailed reporting here, but you will find good resources listed in the appendix. Read them, and practice short hikes at home with your pack on your back.

The frame-type pack is the only suitable means for hauling your gear on a hike. Each of the many pack styles serves its purpose, but settle for nothing less than a properly fitted pack frame. Padded shoulder straps add comfort, and a waist band distributes the weight between the back and hips.

Men should not ordinarily attempt to carry more than 35 pounds for all-day packing; women should limit pack weight to about 25 pounds. The children will want to carry their share, with weight suited to strength.

You can buy a lightweight cook kit, or you can assemble your own by saving various sized cans. The advantage of tin can cookery is simple. You throw the cans away at trip's end! And they cost nothing. If you are careful not to leave them untended over the fire, ordinary cans will serve as well as the commercial cook kits. The #10 can holds about a gallon, all you need for trail camping, with many smaller sizes that nest nicely.

The badge of the hiker is his cup hooked to his belt. I personally find this a nuisance and tuck my cup in a side pocket of my pack. Sometimes in the mountains I carry a folded paper cup in my back pocket. What I lose in sanitation, I make up in convenience. I am getting too old to lie on my belly and drink from a stream as I once did.

One compromise you can make is in your choice of a sleeping bag. Pound for pound, nothing beats goose down filler, but you must pay two or three times as much for a down bag as you would for one with synthetic fibers. If you plan many trips, the down bag will add to your camping pleasure.

I prefer foam pads to air mattresses, and here the cost is about the same. Children often refuse any padding, but this may not be wise. The pad contributes as much to warmth as softness. More body heat is lost through the ground than into the air when no insulation is provided.

Plan your menu carefully. Backpacking allows for few frills. One-pot meals are preferable, with a smaller pot for the coffee if you mistrust the instant variety as I do. Concentrated, high calorie foods are available for noon meals, eliminating the need for cooking.

When you plan a mountain hike, study the route description to learn where firewood is available. In higher altitudes lightweight stoves are required. Several varieties can be purchased which burn petroleum or alcohol fuels. And don't look down on the old-fashioned canned heat stove with jellied alcohol.

Regardless of the kind of trip you plan, rules for health and safety are much alike. Know your equipment and study your route. Topographical maps covering almost every foot of the country can be purchased, and you should understand how to use a compass.

While it is possible to get lost, it is almost impossible to stay lost if you keep your head. In most areas, the best rescue signal is a huge, smoky, controlled fire. Wandering aimlessly in hope of finding your way is foolhardy. You burn up energy and diminish the chances for rescue. Very often a lost person wanders into an area which has been already searched and thus is missed by the rescue team.

9
Happiness Is a Light Pack

Regardless of the terrain or mode of travel, trail camping happiness is a light pack. On the Cascade father-son trip mentioned earlier, I found my saddle horse preempted for pack duty, leaving me on foot. So I elected to be last up the trail to make sure no one lagged. Our base camp lay nine miles away over Twisp Pass, a mild 6,000-foot elevation, as I recall. The day was clear and I enjoyed poking along at my own pace.

About three or four miles up the trail, I came upon three of our campers, a dad and two sons. The boys were perhaps 9 and 11, and they were tired, but not nearly as tired as Dad! He sprawled on the side of the trail and said, "This is ridiculous!" I looked at his pack and agreed.

I had cautioned the hikers to keep their packs light, not more than 35 pounds for the men and bigger boys, 25 pounds or less for the younger lads. I hefted the tired camper's pack. It must have approached 50 pounds with a pair of heavy boots dangling from the frame. I imagine his longest hike in recent years had extended from parking lot to office.

In a moment of weakness I said, "Let me help you for a

while." That recharged the man's batteries. In fact, that was the last I saw of him until we reached camp! I discovered I was not in much better shape than he was. A heavy pack takes all the joy out of hiking, so plan your gear carefully, and leave at home what you do not really need.

Clothes for the Trail Trotter

Novice campers almost always pack too many clothes. The auto camper soon discovers the value of simple living, with regular visits to the laundromat to wash his wash-and-wear garments. The trail camper should limit himself to two changes in addition to the clothes he wears. And he uses the laundromat of the trail, a sturdy plastic bag. A few drops of soap, water from the stream or lake, and vigorous shaking accomplishes wonders for trail-soiled clothes. And who says one must don clean clothes every day? The hard-core, light-pack camper takes one change of clothes and sometimes brings it home unworn!

Several layers of clothing provide greater comfort than bulky sweaters or jackets. A windbreaker, wool sweater, flannel shirt and warm undershirt will conquer unseasonable weather in the summer. Of course, winter camping calls for another strategy.

An added word about footgear is in order. Wear sturdy, well-fitting boots to protect the ankle and arch. *Break them in before the trip!* In spite of repeated cautions, almost every group has at least one camper sporting brand-new boots, shiny and stiff. Blisters are inevitable! More than one camper has been forced to abandon a trip the first day out because he did not properly break in his boots.

The quickest and best way to insure foot comfort is to put your new boots on at home. Soak your feet (with the boots on) in the bathtub for 10 minutes or so, until the boots are thoroughly wet. Then hike until they are dry! Someone is sure to scoff at this, but he has probably never tried it. Water does not harm leather if you do not attempt to dry it with intense heat. Never prop your boots near the fire to dry. They are sure to shrink.

Avoid wearing boots and overshoes of any man-made material. None of them breathe, and your feet will soon perspire and grow uncomfortable. Wear a light pair of socks, perhaps nylon, next to your feet, with a medium-weight wool sock. Rinse out the socks each night, wearing your extra pair the following day. Comfortable feet make for happy camping.

A hat is important to shade you from the sun and to protect your head from insects. An old felt hat is excellent. Buying a fancy cowboy hat is a mistake unless you wear it long enough to feel comfortable. The bulk and broad brim, though romantic looking, are difficult to get used to. Nothing beats the broad-brimmed western hat if you can forget you are wearing it; but break it in, just like your boots.

Rain gear is essential on any extended trip. The poncho has many uses, but protecting a hiker from rain is not one of them. It does fit over a pack, but a lightweight nylon pack cover does the job better. Secure a waist-length, loose-fitting nylon rain jacket. Plastic jackets are a waste of money because they will rip quickly and prove useless. Do not worry if your legs get wet. They will dry. And if you are wearing wool pants, they will keep you reasonably warm even when wet.

Shorts can be worn at times, but not when the bugs are active, or when you are hiking through rough country. Long sleeves are recommended for protection. Carry at least one long-sleeved shirt in addition to your windbreaker. One traditional western item you will find useful is the bandanna. Dress comfortably and sensibly. And keep your clothes sack small!

Guidelines for Planning

If you have had no experience camping in the wilderness, invite a veteran camping family to join you for your first trip. While reading books and magazine articles will prove helpful, you will learn best by observing experienced campers.

Most communities have outdoor gear shops where you can examine equipment. You will discover a wide variety of tastes and opinions among campers as to the best way to camp. The right way is the way that works for you and provides the adventure you seek on the trail.

How much gear is too much? Anything you can get along without should be left at home or in the car. Careful work with one camera lens will compensate for the heavy photo bag left behind. Four or five of the most effective lures in a pocket-size tackle box makes the multitiered fisherman's delight unnecessary. Radios, hair curlers, shoe polish, cosmetics, and firearms do not belong in your pack.

Plan before you pack. Organize your gear into categories and assemble it in one place before beginning to stuff it into packs. Here are suggestions to help you draw up your personal packing list. You must ruthlessly cut the list, or spend days on the trail regretting it.

1. Camping.

• *Tent:* Stakes and poles, if regulations prohibit cutting them along the way. Green shrubs and trees may *never* be used for this purpose. Rain tarp, if your tent requires one.

• *Tools:* Saw or light ax (ax not usually needed if a mallet is provided for driving stakes); sturdy pocketknife or sheath knife; tent repair kit; pliers, screw driver, an extra spark plug, and box of sheer pins if involved with outboard motors.

• *Rope:* Light nylon line is excellent and inexpensive.

• *Plastic sheeting:* 8′ x 10′. Useful for rain cover over firewood, gear, or tent; also as a wind shelter.

2. *Cooking.*

• *Cook kit:* One of the nesting variety; an aluminum griddle, unless on a backpack trip where every ounce is counted; enough plates, cups, and silverware for the party; cooking utensils—large spoon, spatula, fillet knife; old glove for working around fire; a cup-sized throwaway plastic container for desserts, soups, etc. (wash and reuse throughout the trip); ample supply of matches in moisture-proof container (double plastic sandwich bag will do); fire grate.

• *Cleanup:* Biodegradable soap; scouring pads; roll of paper toweling; knit cotton or nylon sack for dipping dishes (allows boiling, but beware of boiling some plastics).

3. *Personal gear.*

• *Clothing:* Two extra changes; windbreaker; sweater; long-sleeve shirt; long pants; shorts (for warm, bugless days on clear trail); hat; comfortable hiking boots; loafers or sneakers for camp wear; wool socks; rain gear (light nylon, loose-fitting). Pack each person's clothes in a plastic or rubberized bag with name displayed.

• *Sleeping bag:* Three-pound synthetic filler adequate for most summer trips; extra blanket for cold weather; foam pad (better than an air mattress), 48-inch length adequate. Ground cloth under tents contributes to comfort. Use rolled-up sweater for pillow, or life vest if traveling by boat or canoe.

• *Personal effects:* Chapstick; sun lotion; glasses holder (elastic band around head); medications and personal hygiene needs; toothbrush; towel and soap; razor (if needed); sleeping clothes or pajamas; mosquito lotion; nonpolluting bug spray; toilet paper.

• *Miscellaneous:* Camera and film; binoculars; sewing kit (needles, nylon thread, buttons, safety pins, razor blade or small scissors); first aid kit (antiseptic, elastic bandage, gauze, Band-Aids, tweezers, burn ointment, laxative, Kaopectate, aspirin, compact first aid manual, fever thermometer, baking soda, long-nosed pliers if on fishing trip; flashlight; spare batteries and bulb; maps (protected in plastic from rain); compass; trail guides; emergency match supply.

4. Foods. Because the selection and preparation of meals is such a large part of trail camping, a special section will be devoted to this. When backpacking, food packets will be distributed among all the hikers. Canoe and pack animal trips ordinarily include special food packs.

Organizing the Packs

Having assembled everything for the packs, plan carefully to keep handy those items most frequently used along the trail. Try to repack the same way each time, and soon you will find it easy to locate sweaters, rain gear, maps, rope, and the noon lunch—saving much time and nervous energy for small emergencies that arise.

Secure your compass to your belt with a line, or buy a wrist or pin-on model. Practice orienting your map with the compass, and always note the general lay of the land and your planned direction of travel. Advance thinking on these matters must be part of your trip planning.

Fit each pack to the family member who is to carry it and practice hiking with the pack in place. Selective packing comes only with experience. In spite of great care, almost every camper finds he has carried much more than he actually needed. Evaluate your gear following every outing. Determine how frequently each item was used, and what substitute might have been employed. Make notes to discipline yourself the next time you pack. Beware of impulse packing; the random item you think might come in handy might be a bothersome extra.

Remember the limits: 35 pounds for men, 25 for women, 25 or less for children depending on age and development. Sure, you can carry more. But at day's end you will wish you had left some of it behind.

Create your own packing system. Do not trust your memory. Write down your list and stick to it. The obvious item often stays home because everyone assumed the other person remembered it.

Comforts and Cautions on the Trail

An incredibly few years ago, wilderness living was the normal pattern for our forefathers. When you visit a restored old settler's cabin, you will be impressed that the pioneer made peace with his environment. He lived from the forest and fields, bending with each season. He felt the wilderness to be inexhaustible.

He gave no thought to the hardship of sleeping out under the sky or perhaps building a brush shelter. He cooked his fish and game over coals, found his way through unmapped wilderness, and kept a wary eye out for enemies, animal or human. Even so, he faced no danger to match our freeways!

Before him the Indian owned the land for generations, before white men stole it. The Indian knew a hard life, but what life he enjoyed came from the wilderness. He would smile at some of the fears novice campers bring to their camps.

Today we turn our backs on the city to seek a wilderness retreat. Each year it becomes harder to find solitude, and unless those who use the wilds change their attitudes, we will be the last generation to have a wilderness.

Feeding the Family

Trail cooking can be as simple or fancy as you choose, but remember that fancy cooking takes time. Most backpack meals should be the one-pot variety, for your cooking gear will be limited. Reflector ovens or the aluminum Dutch ovens make campfire baking feasible, but breads can be prepared in simpler ways.

Techniques for cooking over an open fire demand more space than we can allow here, so check the books listed in the bibliography, and practice cooking at home! Build a fire in the outdoor grill to learn how to control the heat by the use of small limbs or finely split wood.

Once you learn to manage your cooking fire, you can qualify as an expert camp chef, for the major difference between home and camp cooking is the source of heat. The rule for the cooking fire is this: use the least fire possible to do the job. Where hardwoods are available, your problem is simplified: Build a bed of coals that gives off steady heat throughout meal preparation. But much wilderness in the North offers mainly soft woods—cedar, pine, spruce or fir. These, along with aspen, disappear into light ash with only brief lives as coals. You must feed the fire with fresh wood regularly.

Take enough time to build a secure base for your cooking pots. Never place them directly on the fire, though the right size logs placed parallel can be used when you have gained experience. A good solution for this problem is a portable grate which you level on a stone fireplace. Many campsites provide cooking grills built by the forestry service.

Firewood can usually be found with no trouble if you hike 100 yards or so from camp. While canoe camping, paddle down the shore away from the camp, then walk into the woods out of sight from the lake to preserve the integrity of the shoreline. I have never failed to find all the firewood I could use, and tent poles as well, with far less effort than gleaning the area adjacent to the camp which every camper explores.

When firewood is discussed, the camp ax comes to mind. The ax tradition dies hard, but you do not really need one. Carry a mallet for driving tent stakes and a bow saw, those marvelous tools with tough blades that will cut more wood with less effort than any ax ever invented. Under certain conditions the ax is invaluable, but camping families can remove one of the major sources of accidents if they leave the ax at home. A hand ax can be more dangerous than the long-handled variety.

Firewood presents a problem in the high country, and in some areas, open fires may be prohibited. Determine this prior to your trip and provide alternatives for cooking. Several lightweight camp stoves burning gasoline, kerosine, or alcohol can be purchased. If the trip is brief and weight is not a problem, a sack of charcoal will do. (Most campers use entirely too much charcoal when cooking.) But when conditions permit, the smell of coffee simmering alongside a pan of frying fish over an open fire makes camping worthwhile all by itself.

Trail Camp Menu

Feeding the family away from the supermarket is not as difficult as you might think. Several firms stand ready to serve you with complete menus packaged for two, four, or six persons. Packets are complete right down to measuring bags and scouring pads for cleanup. There are no problems of refrigeration, trash disposal, or breakage.

If you have not tried dehydrated and freeze-dried foods for several years, you are in for a happy surprise. The taste and ease of preparation has improved greatly. The variety of camping meals has broadened from the days of canned beans to include scrambled eggs, cocoa, pudding, macaroni and cheese, chicken à la king, gelatin, turkey, mixed vegetables, and even beef stroganoff with noodles.

Care should be taken to measure water accurately for packaged foods. Usually you will need five minutes extra for simmering than is called for on the package. All cooking

SEVEN-DAY MENU

	1st Day	2d Day	3d Day	4th Day	5th Day	6th Day	7th Day
Breakfast							
	Bacon and Eggs, Toast, Tang, Coffee or Cocoa	French Toast, Bacon, Syrup, Tang, Coffee or Cocoa	Pancakes, Syrup, Grapefruit Juice, Coffee or Cocoa	Scrambled Eggs, Bacon Bar, Toast, Tang, Coffee, Cocoa	Cooked Cereal, Stewed Fruit, Toast, Coffee or Cocoa	Western Omelet, Toast, Tang, Coffee, Cocoa	French Toast, Syrup, Juice, Coffee, Cocoa
Lunch							
	Salami Sandwich, Candy Bars, Beverage	American Cheese, Crackers, Jelly, Cookies, Beverage	Summer Sausage Sandwich, Candy Bar, Beverage	Jelly Spread, Bolten Biscuits, Raisins, Cookies, Beverage	Cheddar Cheese Crackers, Mixed Fruit, Beverage	Peanut Butter, Jelly Sandwich, Cookies, Beverage	American Cheese Sandwich, Jelly, Raisins, Candy Bars, Beverage
Dinner							
	Fresh Beef Patties (groups) or Chicken, Fresh Steaks (individuals) or Chicken. Hash Browns, Peas and Carrots, Gelatin Dessert, Beverage	Ham and Potato Dinner, Green Beans, Pudding, Beverage	Deluxe Beef Stew, Hot Biscuits, Applesauce, Beverage	Beef Stroganoff with Noodles, Peas, Cobbler Dessert, Beverage	Chicken ala King, Hot Biscuits, Corn, Mashed Potatoes, Gelatin Dessert, Beverage	Spaghetti, Mixed Vegetables, Chocolate Pie, Beverage	Beef and Spuds, Carrots, Rice Pudding, Beverage

94

instructions are printed on the package, so remember not to burn the box until the cooking is finished!

If you enjoy planning meals on your own, visit the packaged food section of your market. List available main dishes, dried soups, and instant desserts. Remember your cooking limitations. Do not come up with a meal that requires slow baking for two hours! Of course, you can use a reflector oven or Dutch oven, but both are time-consuming.

The foods mentioned above are lightweight with burnable packaging. The weight will run about 20 ounces per person per day. If you have ever packed a week's canned food through the mountains, you will appreciate the difference. Many wilderness areas forbid the use of canned or bottled foods.

As you plan each day's menu, write down the needs for each meal. Remember to include such items as seasonings, shortening, condiments, and an extra touch for bedtime snacks. Hot chocolate and marshmallows are a favorite. Popcorn is less easily prepared with the usual camp pots, but it can be done. Even cookies and fruit drink will send the children to the tent happy.

Camp Feeding Kinks

It is a good idea to add dried fruits for snacks. Small packages of raisins provide energy during the day. Bowel irregularities are common when the diet changes substantially, and fruit is useful for good health and dispositions. Remember too that calorie needs for campers exceed those required at home.

Cooking gear has been mentioned elsewhere, but check your menu carefully, keeping in mind the pots and pans available. One of those collapsible plastic water jugs, 2½ or 5 gallon, will spare your largest pot for cooking if you must store water in the camp. Remember cooking utensils and a cleanup kit including scouring pads and dish soap.

Clean dishes provide a defense against one of the most common camp ailments—upset stomach. Often this results from soiled or unrinsed dishes. Rinse the dishes thoroughly, and always use biodegradable soaps.

With the growing number of campers, you should exercise care with the drinking water even in areas where waters have not been polluted. Purifying pellets can be purchased, but you must allow sufficient time for them to work. Boiling any beverage automatically solves the problem. Adding fruit flavoring to drinking water masks the taste of purifying elements which some find unpleasant.

Food storage presents another problem. Most packaged foods need no additional care, but some foods must be kept cool. Toting a cooler through the woods is impractical, except for canoe trips which require few portages. A large burlap or cloth sack will serve. Place the food to be cooled in watertight plastic, place the plastic bag in the cloth sack, and soak it thoroughly. Hang the sack in the shade where the breeze can hit it, and evaporation will maintain a temperature low enough to preserve even fish fillets all day. This method usually keeps food cooler than placing it in the water, unless you are near a spring or mountain stream.

The Wilderness Home

Lightweight tents are available at fairly reasonable prices, though good quality in all backpack equipment is essential. You will discover the problem with waterproof nylon tents the first morning in camp. Condensation collects in spite of ventilating windows. Coated nylon fabrics, while wonderfully light, do not breathe as cotton tent cloth does. This is also true of plastic shelters, which appeal because of extremely low prices. Avoid them for serious camping.

Many campers continue to use cotton fabrics, installing a

waterproof fly over the tent when rain threatens. The variety of fabrics and styles available through camp suppliers will allow you to choose the lightweight tent that suits your needs.

Be sure the ground is fairly level and free of stubble or rocks. You will not be packing a cot! A foam pad provides insulation and padding, but a hump in the small of your back makes sleep difficult.

A nylon fly is worth its weight for family trips. Should rain fall for long periods, you can keep dry without huddling in the small tent, and you can cook comfortably and keep gear out of the rain.

The question of wild animal dangers inevitably arises when wilderness camping is discussed. Anyone who has worked with large domestic animals knows that animals, like humans, come with all kinds of dispositions. You can find maniacs among both men and beasts. The two most commonly feared creatures are snakes and bears.

With normal precautions, snake dangers can be minimized. If you tease a snake, he will bite. If you surprise a rattler, he will first try to flee, but he will strike if he finds no way to escape.

In some parts of the country, you need to guard against toxic insects and poisonous plants, but these are just circumstances of life on the trail. Mosquitoes and flies are more of a nuisance than other bugs, and can be controlled by repellent. Learn to identify the toxic plants such as poison ivy and oak.

If you camp in an area inhabited by bears, hang your food packs out of reach. But hang them high! If you can reach them, so can the bear!

Devising a system to outsmart raccoons will tax your ingenuity. They readily open coolers and unlocked food lockers. A suspended pack that thwarts a hungry bear leaves Mr. Raccoon undaunted. Use a thin rope or wire which he cannot negotiate. Be on guard against squirrels and mice too.

On a hunting trip in Alaska, a squirrel carried away every slice of bread we had, leaving us to the mercy of our sourdough starter and flour sack.

Never leave food in your tent, not even candy treats. Cosmetics and toothpaste have been known to attract bears also. A hungry bear will not respect your zippered tent. He will enter and depart by different routes, leaving your tent a shambles, and he will carry your food with him.

It is easy to overdramatize animal dangers in the woods. The chances of encountering anything larger than a squirrel are low. There is no firm evidence that either the black bear or the wolf has ever stalked a man to harm him. Grizzly bears occasionally seem to attack out of sheer spite, but you will rarely see one, even when traveling in their home areas.

The natural instinct of all animals is to flee man. If they feel threatened, or if their escape route is blocked, they may appear to be attacking simply because you are in their way. Almost all female beasts will attack if they think their young are in danger.

Probably the most dangerous bear is the one that discovers the good taste of campers' food. Bears visit the garbage dumps regularly and become accustomed to observers. Some foolish tourist invariably gets too close while taking a picture and the bear reacts, just as a dog reacts if someone tries to take away his food.

Some male animals become dangerous during mating season. Bull moose which are normally docile will sometimes rush people or anything that moves, including automobiles. They have been known to charge locomotives on the Alaskan Railroad!

Most encounters with animals in camp are related to their desire for your menu, especially when natural food is not plentiful. You can sleep peacefully if you observe the cautions mentioned above. Never, in hundreds of nights over many years, has my sleep been broken by an animal seeking shelter in my tent.

The Wilderness Ethic

Family camping is an excellent way to teach children the importance of conservation. Concern for ecology is no mere fad. Human survival depends on mankind making peace with his environment. Surely, the Christian should take the lead in exercising good stewardship over the earth.

Building bough beds, erecting pioneer-type bridges and towers, ditching tents, burying garbage: All these belong to the careless past.

A view of the camper's relation to the wilderness has been well stated by Gerry Cunningham of the Colorado Outdoors Sports Company of Denver, Colorado:

Wilderness camping is an experience basically different from pioneer camping, although there are similarities.

The usual camp program and the majority of camping books still teach the *Pioneering Ethic*. Skill with the ax, knife, and saw; the construction of some of the comforts of civilization within the wilderness is the gist of most. These programs are variously labeled campcraft, trailcraft, pioneering, or survival. Almost all such activities leave their mark on the wilderness, some small ineradicable evidence that man has passed this way.

The time has come to realize that we no longer need to pioneer and subdue the wilderness. The time has come to start teaching the *Wilderness Ethic,* which says that man should pass through the wilderness as unobtrusively as the animals do, leaving no sign of his passing. In fact, man's technology has progressed to the point where he can carry a far more comfortable camp on his back than he can build out of the wilderness.

The true wilderness traveler will camp where no one has camped before, and leave no evidence of his temporary use of God's country. Under these conditions, the wilderness will support many many more users than it does at present, and with increased enjoyment by more people will come the guarantee of its preservation.

Wilderness Traveler's Code

I will keep my group small. Large herds of animals or people leave lasting evidence, if they stay too long in one place.

I will not build bough beds or other campcraft projects. There is no need for bough beds with modern sleeping equipment, and any display of axmanship to build lean-tos, picnic tables, and camp kitchen paraphernalia is entirely out of keeping with appreciation of the wilderness.

I will protect the ground cover. This is one of the most delicate parts of the wilderness. Such activities as ditching tents, burying garbage, and clearing fire circles destroy in minutes what it may have taken 100 years to build up.

I will use small fires. A small Indian fire made of squaw wood that can be picked up off the ground and broken in your hands will be much more comfortable to cook on and leave a minimum of evidence when you leave. Instead of clearing a large spot on the forest floor for a safe fire, it is easier to build up such an area on top of the forest floor with mineral dirt or gravel. The few rocks used to confine such a fire can be scattered with the dead charcoal when you leave. This will remove all traces of your camp.

I will leave no trash. Everything was carried in. If it cannot be burned, it can be carried back out again. Don't throw it in the bushes and don't bury it. Garbage and plastic and paper can be burned. Aluminum foil and cans must be carried out.

Some travelers won't have been as careful of the wilderness as you are, so when you find their cans and paper, pick 'em up and pack 'em out.

Trail trips strengthen the spiritual potential inherent in all family camping. Out there away from traffic and people, the family shares life with an intimacy not found elsewhere. A latrine in the bush becomes a certain equalizer. So does the crowded backpack tent. Families learn that the sophistications common to urban life are quite unnecessary. They can live openly and simply.

When you plan a family trip into the back country, allow time for worship. This may prove to be the most authentic worship your family ever experiences, for life on the trail does not lend itself to empty ritual. Spiritual values emerge from the hearts of people who discover the real presence of Christ within.

NOTE: Some of the material in this chapter was adapted from *Family Camping* by Lloyd Mattson, Moody Press.

10
Trail Devotions

The lesson of the trail is a total life experience. Bible study, personal devotions, campfire sharing and one-on-one counseling become integral parts of the day. The attitude and character of the parents make up much of the spiritual instruction.

If it is true that learning requires participation in the subject matter, then few situations can compare with trail camping as an environment for Christian education, for Christianity is primarily a way of life. The Bible is the guidebook for Christian living. On the trail, life is basic and urgent, and quite different from life at home. The prospects for learning grow as difficulties and delights multiply. The glory of God's Gospel can be discovered readily as campers observe parents in action. This observation imposes on parents the responsibility to provide the right kind of example.

Proper devotional guidance requires recognition of the natures and limitations of family members. The setting too must be considered. Most youngsters have a limited attention span. Most will be concerned about now, not eternity.

Practical matters concern them, rather than philosophical; people are more important to them than impersonal principles or systems.

Trail devotions then should focus on the personal issues of the Gospel, with a controlled input of ideas to allow for maximum impact, through planned repetition. The devotions outlined below have been tested on many trail trips, usually with success. No method serves every group equally well, so flexibility and adaptability must be applied according to the group's needs. Simplicity, repetition, participation: These are the key words for planning effective wilderness Bible discovery for the family.

The basic principle is emphasized in one story or Bible portion throughout the day, and focused on a key verse. No overt pressure for memorizing the verse is necessary, for repetition through the day will impress the words on the memory.

If youngster and parents absorb one spiritual principle each day, this is no small accomplishment! If the camper applies one life-changing principle to himself during a trip, few would consider the devotional effort a failure. It's not how much a camper hears, but what he grasps that measures the success of any teaching.

• *Bible Exploration* at some time in the morning; weather, bugs and travel conditions permitting. The question: *What is God saying to the world in this Bible passage?*

• *Reflection Time* after lunch, or during an afternoon rest stop, can be one-by-one, or sometimes two-by-two. Point to the Bible passage explored in the morning. The question: *What is God saying to me in this passage?*

• *Campfire Sharing* in the evening. Pace the day to allow time and energy for this. Return to the same Bible passage with the question: *What happened today?*

Bible Exploration

Bible Exploration is a guided tour: A given Bible passage or story contains specific teachings plus many inferences or applications. Bible Exploration leads the camper into the passage and encourages him to isolate the ideas or make applications. The guide will often be surprised with the findings!

The Bible Exploration guide does not "teach," though he may provide needed background not explicit in the passage. He manages the group process so no one dominates or withdraws. He may nudge campers toward a discovery through careful questions or casually dropped ideas.

Here is a pattern for Bible Exploration:

1. Read the portion. Every person should have a Bible, preferably a New Testament. Large Bibles are difficult to manage on the trail.

2. Provide essential background. Don't retell the story or outline the points, but give the setting and explain unusual words or circumstances. Put the passage into a meaningful context for the family. Don't preach!

3. Ask the question, "What is God saying to the world through this passage?"

Having read the Bible account, spend a few minutes with the key verse. Read it in unison two or three times. This verse will often become the principle discovery area as it is repeated throughout the day.

Teach campers how to pray the verse back to God; repeating each phrase, giving thanks for a blessing, claiming a promise, submitting to a command, confessing a failure. Provide this model for the camper's prayer during Reflection Time.

Preparation for leading Bible Exploration is no less demanding than preparation for the traditional teaching pattern. Perhaps it is more demanding, for the leader can never be certain which direction the group will move. The leader must be thoroughly familiar with the passage and its background.

Understanding something about the setting of a Bible story helps the camper grasp its meaning. The location, nature and background of the first readers; customs of Bible times; identity of the writer; and any other information that will bring the passage into focus will prove useful. But beware of consuming too much time with background.

A Bible passage has *one* meaning, many applications. Search for the meaning, and don't dogmatize on the applications. The meaning of the story to each camper will vary according to his circumstances. Parables are ordinarily explained by other Scripture. Pressing for each detail can create difficulties. The question for Bible Exploration is simply: "What is God saying to the world through this passage? What does it mean?"

Securing participation may prove difficult at first, since we are conditioned by church custom to listen passively while the leader talks. You may find it necessary to ask direct questions. But remember that you are not teaching a "lesson," but leading a discovery expedition.

How long should a devotional session last? This will vary. When you search for something, you quit when you find it, or when the prospects for discovery are exhausted. It's the same with Bible Exploration. Try to close the session while interest remains high. Leave some ideas undeveloped for meditation. You can trust God's Spirit to continue the teaching.

Bring together the main ideas put forth in discussion, but don't preach! Let ideas percolate in the campers' hearts. You may wish to hint at one or two key thoughts overlooked in discussion. Review suggestions for the day's Reflection Time. Assign prayer partners if this is your practice. Recite the key verse in unison one more time and close with prayer.

Reflection Time

Reflection Time asks the camper to review the Bible passage explored earlier in the day. Occasionally, circumstances may have forced you to omit Bible Exploration. Then you must judge whether a group session should be conducted, or the Reflection Time pattern followed.

Reflection Time should cover at least 10 minutes, with additional time available for those who wish to continue. A 30-minute break following lunch, or an afternoon pause provides a logical time. The maturity of your group will determine whether you send campers off individually or two-by-two. Generally, the less mature campers will benefit from being teamed up with a mature person.

The basics for Reflection Time are:

1. Read again the Bible passage explored earlier, or a parallel passage.

2. Ask, "What does God say to *me* through this passage? How does it speak to my problem or meet my need?"

3. Pray the portion back to God, thought by thought, particularly the key verse. Then have personal prayer, including subjects selected by the group and by prayer mates.

The temptation will be strong to neglect Reflection Time, just as the pace of everyday life causes many Christians to neglect private prayer and meditation. While adverse weather or other circumstances may force postponement of either a meal or Reflection Time, the day should be planned to include both!

Campfire Sharing

Plan the campfire when the evening activity is over and camp chores are finished. Everyone should participate in singing, sharing the day's events, evaluation of adventures: a blending of family interests.

Help youngsters participate by asking nonthreatening questions: "What happened that was funny? Thrilling? Who caught the biggest fish? Did you learn anything new?" Guide the mood toward devotional thoughts through songs or by quoting the day's key verse. Then ask the question, "What happened in your heart?"

Responses should never be forced. Perhaps nothing of significance occurred, or perhaps a camper is not yet ready to talk about it. A camper may be asked in advance to share a story, or an account of his spiritual growth.

Campfires should be relaxed and brief. The fire should be kindled in advance, with an adequate supply of firewood on hand. In some areas campfires cannot be built because of fire hazard or lack of firewood. This does not prevent an evening group gathering, perhaps around a lantern and with a shared snack.

Far North campers may not wish to wait for darkness. Some camps find the sharing time most practical following supper. Flexibility and creative use of time allows the leader to make whatever adjustments are needed to gain the spiritual values he seeks. At some time during the day, opportunity should be given for campers to share their spiritual encounters. The campfire provides a rich setting for this.

Further Tips for Effective Trail Devotions

1. Preparation: Every devotional leader should be thoroughly familiar with the material and devotional philosophy. He should be equipped to guide the exploration rather than teach a lesson.

2. Adaptation: Meet the specific needs of the group rather than following the letter of the materials. Adapt both content and format to the spiritual maturity of the campers.

3. Flexibility: Adjust to the contingencies of trail life:

weather, bugs, emergencies. Remember that the spiritual impact of a trip grows out of the total experience, not just the devotional program.

4. *Simplicity:* The depth of experience holds priority over the volume of content. Deal with basic needs. Practice elementary devotional skills: prayer, sharing, thoughtful Bible reading.

5. *Pray-back:* Teach the skill of praying God's Word back to Him as a means for reinforcing learning and gaining personal involvement with the Bible message.

6. *Brevity:* Cultivate the spirit of constant awareness of God's presence, while keeping formal sessions brief. When interest lags, the leader must share the blame.

7. *Repetition:* Use one key verse a day, one passage for exploration a day. Explore, reflect, share: three opportunities for guiding the camper into the Word.

8. *Dependence:* Only God's Spirit can accomplish God's work. Leaders guide campers into the Word. The Spirit supplies, convicts, converts, and convinces. It's hard to hear God speaking when men make too much noise.

LEADER'S GUIDE

CHRIST ON THE MOUNTAINS

The country where Jesus lived is a small and rugged land of contrasts—with towering mountains and the lowest spot on earth. Mt. Hermon reaches 9,200 feet, while the Dead Sea shore is 1,292 feet below sea level. The deepest spot in the Dead Sea drops another 1,300 feet!

Jerusalem is some 2,550 feet above sea level and the Mt. of Olives is 2,680. The mountain ridge running north and south between the sea coast and the Jordan River makes travel on foot a demanding experience, with the series of valleys common to such terrain.

Often the term *mountain* in the Bible could better be translated "hill," as it is in newer versions. Jesus chose the hills and mountains for much of His ministry, partly because they afforded a measure of seclusion when He needed it, and partly because the hills and mountains were simply there.

Those who love to hike the mountains understand Jesus' selection of the high country. A study of the events that occurred on the mountains in the life of Jesus is especially fitting for the trail devotions series.

1. Mountain of Temptation—Matthew 4:1-11. (See also Mark 1:12-13; Luke 4:1-13; Hebrews 4:15.)

Key verse: Matthew 4:4

Check points:

- Who led Jesus into the wilderness? (v. 1)
- Were Jesus' temptations real? (Hebrews 4:15) Hunger: bread. New ministry: He needed an audience. Revolutionary claim: He needed authority. The temptations were real!
- How did Jesus answer Satan? (The Word)
- Can Satan use Scripture? (v. 6)
- Is it wrong to take shortcuts to achieve good ends?
- What basic human needs did Satan appeal to? Physical (food). Psychological (attention, acceptance). Social (leadership, power).

2. Mountain of Instruction—Matthew 5:1-16. (See also Luke 6:20-45.)

Key verse: Matthew 5:16

Check points:

- The primary audience was the Twelve, with the crowd looking on. The setting was a hillside, deliberately chosen in order to withdraw from the public. Jesus set forth His teachings about the godly life—not how one becomes a child of God, but how God's child should live.

• The Beatitudes contain a list of personal qualities that mark the Christian life. See also 1 Corinthians 13; Galatians 5:22-23; 2 Peter 1:5-7. Note parallels.

• How should a Christian react to unfair criticism? (v. 11)

• Think of the various values of salt. Remember that salt creates thirst.

• Why should the Christian display a godly life? (v. 16)

3. Mountain of Appointment—Luke 6:12-16. (See also Mark 3:13-19.)

Key verse: Mark 3:14

Jesus had many dedicated followers. From the many, He chose twelve for special assignment and training. Not everyone was called in the same way.

Check points:

• What preceded the appointment of the Twelve? (all-night prayer)

• Is there a difference between an apostle and a disciple? (Apostle: a sent one, missionary. Disciple: a learner, follower.)

• Were the Twelve perfect men?

• Note in the key verse the sequence: Jesus appointed the Twelve to be *with* Him, and then to be *sent out* to preach. Spending time with Jesus must precede service.

4. Mountain of Provision—John 6:1-14. (See also Matthew 14:13-21; Luke 9:10-17.)

Key verse: John 6:9

Check points:

• What does the story tell about Jesus' concern for human needs?

• Jesus used a lad's resources as the basic material out of which He fed the crowd, though He had the power to make bread out of stones. What does this suggest? (God asks that we yield what we possess for His purpose, no matter how inadequate our possessions may seem to us.)

• Was Jesus' provision adequate?

• What were the disciples' reactions to Jesus' proposal to feed the crowd? (vv. 7-8)

• Who was the lad? There is no data and much speculation. Whether his lunch, or bread and fish were for sale is uncertain. Regardless, the boy surrendered all he had to Jesus and received many times more in return.

• What does the story imply concerning the surrender of our lives to Jesus? (Enough for His purpose, with blessing abounding.)

5. *Mountain of Transfiguration—Mark 9:2-8.* (See also Matthew 17:1-8; Luke 9:28-36.)

Key verse: Mark 9:8

Check points:

• Who accompanied Jesus to the mountain? (Peter, James, John. They were chosen several times for special encounters and became the most prominent among the Twelve.)

• Who appeared on the mountain? (Moses, the lawgiver; Elijah, the prophet.)

• The three disciples wanted to build three shrines. What was wrong with that idea? (Moses and Elijah did not belong on the same level as Jesus. God was no longer working through the temple or man-built shrines, but in the hearts of people.)

• What was the statement and command from heaven? (Mark 9:7)

• What is the provocative thought found in Mark 9:8?

6. *Mountain of Commissioning—Matthew 28:16-20.* (See also Acts 1:6-12.)

Key verse: Matthew 28:19-20

Check points:

• Though Matthew 28:16-20 and Acts 1:6-12 are related in

concept, they are separate events. You may want to look at both, pointing out that the Acts passage occurs on the Mountain of Ascension.

• How did the Disciples respond when they saw Jesus? (Worship and doubt, common to all Christians.)

• How did Jesus respond to worship and doubt? (He spoke: God's Word is enough.)

• How much authority does Jesus possess? (All, in heaven and earth.)

• What command does Jesus give? (Make disciples: "Go" in this verse is not a command, but a factor accompanying the command. Not all may go to some far place. All can make disciples.)

• How much of the world did Jesus mention? (All nations . . . the whole world.)

• What are the parts of the Great Commission? (Make disciples, baptize, teach. Full obedience must include all three.)

• What special promise did Jesus include in the Commission? (With you always.)

The Camper's Log on the following pages may be duplicated in simple form to guide the camper in personal devotions.

CAMPER'S LOG

CHRIST ON THE MOUNTAINS

Welcome to the mountain trails with the Master. Jesus spent much time on the hills and mountains of His homeland. We will think about some of those high experiences and see what He will teach us.

Some of life's most important lessons will be considered in Bible Exploration and Reflection Time. If you take the challenge of this study seriously, you can find a new direction for your life.

Follow each suggestion in your Camper's Log. Read reflectively the key verse. Think about its personal message to you. Pray back its ideas to the Author. Reflect on God's calling to you.

Remember your trailmate each day, learning the ministry of intercessory prayer. Share in the assigned prayer work. Seek something to share with others each day when opportunity comes.

Ask the Lord to make camp a life-changing adventure for you.

I. MOUNTAIN OF TEMPTATION Matthew 4:1-11

Key verse: "Man shall not live on bread alone, but on every word that proceeds out of the mouth of God" (Matthew 4:4, NASB).

Think it over: If Jesus needed God's Word as a defense

against Satan, how about me? How about the temptation to take shortcuts to what appear to be reasonable goals?

Pray-back: Lord, help me learn that physical goals alone are not enough for a meaningful life. Help me live by Your Word. Thank You for the Bible which You gave.

Your own words: What spoke to your heart during Bible Exploration? Do you have thoughts or plans you should talk over with the Lord? Are you willing to pass up what appear to be advantages when the means used are questionable?

Trailmate: _____

Prayer work: _____

Ideas for sharing: _____

II. MOUNTAIN OF INSTRUCTION Matthew 5:1-16

Key verse: "Let your light shine before men in such a way that they may see your good works, and glorify your Father who is in heaven" (Matthew 5:16, NASB).

Think it over: How many people find me a blessing? Whose life is more rewarding and flavorful because he knows me? Has anyone seen God's light through me?

Pray-back: Talk each phrase and idea of the key verse over with the Lord: your light, your good works, God's glory. How do your life and attitudes measure up?

Your own words: What idea from the Bible Exploration meant most to you? Can you identify some area of your life you should work on in order that you may become more useful to God?

Trailmate: _____

Prayer work: _____

Ideas for sharing: _____

III. MOUNTAIN OF APPOINTMENT Luke 6:12-16

Key verse: "And He appointed Twelve, that they might be with Him, and that He might send them out to preach" (Mark 3:14, NASB).

Think it over: God invites everyone to become a disciple of Jesus. God calls some to special work. What about me?

Pray-back: Lord, thank You that You appoint some for special duty. And thank You that we all can be *with* You as preparation for whatever service You assign. What assignment do You have for my life?

Your own words: God doesn't call all of us to a church-related vocation. Are those who are called more important than those who remain in everyday jobs?

Trailmate: _____

Prayer work: _____

Ideas for sharing: _____

IV. MOUNTAIN OF PROVISION John 6:1-14

Key verse: "There is a lad here who has five barley loaves and two fish, but what are these for so many people?" (John 6:9, NASB).

Think it over: What does Jesus choose to use for His work? What does He require from me? What if I don't seem to have much to offer?

Pray-back: You're on your own from this Reflection Time on. Think carefully through the key verse, and talk over every idea you find in it with the Lord.

Your own words: Pray about the thoughts that came to you as you read the Bible passage, and the ideas that came up in Bible Exploration. Perhaps the Lord will give you insights that will be helpful to the others. Ask Him to give you something special to share.

Trailmate: _____

Prayer work: _____

Ideas for sharing: _____

V. MOUNTAIN OF TRANSFIGURATION Mark 9:2-8

Key verse: "And all at once they looked around and saw no one with them anymore, except Jesus alone" (Mark 9:8, NASB).

Think it over: How do I see Jesus? Do I sort of take Him for granted? Do I need to consider again who He is? How do I see Jesus in relation to others?

Pray-back: Talk over the main point in the key verse. It's a vital point to pray about! We must see Jesus as God's only Son, our Saviour.

Your own words: How about shrine-building? Do we feel our spiritual needs are fulfilled by religious programs and places? Where does God's Spirit dwell?

Trailmate: _____

Prayer work: _____

Ideas for sharing: _____

VI. MOUNTAIN OF COMMISSIONING Matthew 28:16-20

Key verse: "Go therefore and make disciples of all the nations, baptizing them in the name of the Father and the Son and the Holy Spirit, teaching them to observe all that I commanded you; and lo, I am with you always, even to the end of the age" (Matthew 28:19-20, NASB).

Think it over: God cares about the whole world. Do I? God wants me to become more than an ordinary Christian. Am I growing?

Pray-back: A big job! One of the most important verses in the Bible to master.

Your own words: God's world-wide, varied work requires many kinds of workers. Where do you fit into His plan? Pray for guidance to discover God's assignment for your life.

Trailmate: _____

Prayer work: _____

Ideas for sharing: _____

Review your Camper's Log. What important ideas did you gain through reflections and exploration? Plan to share them.

Resources for the Camping Family

Persons interested in reading about outdoor adventure will find a vast and growing literature covering almost every area of interest. We will describe a few of the books we have found helpful. A trip to your local library will probably produce many of these titles, plus others. As special outdoor interests develop, a family will want to build a selected library for broadening skills and enriching the days between trips afield. Most people who enjoy the outdoor life also enjoy reading the experiences of others who live outdoors.

Periodicals

Each outdoor interest has its magazines, and since titles come and go, you will find it helpful to check with your outdoor supplier and library for current periodicals. General magazines such as *Sports Afield* and *Field and Stream* are too well-known to need mention. Several national and regional family camping periodicals will serve the RV campers.

Associations

Denominational and interdenominational family camping fellowships offer resources to the camping family. Local chapters serve the regional interests of those who belong to national organizations. Associations we are acquainted with are:

Campers on Mission, Special Mission Ministries, Home Missions Board, 1350 Spring Street N.W., Atlanta, Georgia 30309.

Christian Family Camping Association, Box 562, Pontiac, Michigan 48058.

Lutheran Family Campers Association, Box 84, Narberth, Pennsylvania 19072.

Camping Club of America, 996 National Press Building, Washington, D.C. 20004.

National Campers and Hikers Association, 7172 Transit Road, Buffalo, New York 14221.

North American Family Campers Association, Box 308, Newbury, Massachusetts 01950.

Christian Camping International, Box 400, Somonauk, Illinois 60056 (an association serving more than a thousand Christian camps and conferences in the U.S. and Canada). For a list of family programs offered in your area, write to Christian Camping International.

Trails-a-Way Caravans, 9731 Riverside Drive, Greenville, Michigan 48838. (Though serving the upper Midwest region primarily, Trails-a-Way conducts camping caravans that will appeal to families everywhere. The monthly *Trails-a-Way* newspaper is delightful, helpful reading for families that enjoy RV camping and outdoor adventure in general.)

Camping Books

Every outdoor enthusiast has his or her favorite author. Ours is Calvin Rutstrum. His intimate, first-hand knowledge of the outdoors and his delightful literary style make all his titles worthwhile. We list only three of them in the special interest categories.

The New Way of the Wilderness, Calvin Rutstrum, The Macmillan Co., New York. Common sense camping skills.

Complete Book of Camping, Leonard Miracle with Maurice H. Decker, *Outdoor Life* Harper & Row, New York. Written some years ago, but still valuable.

The Complete Book of Practical Camping, John Jobson, Winchester Press, New York. Written in 1974, this book updates concepts found in the older books, discussing some of the newer approaches to outdoor living. Good section on motorized travel on and off the road.

Field Book for Boys and Men, Boy Scouts of America. For diversity and practicality, it's hard to beat the Scouting field manual.

The Sierra Club Wilderness Handbook, Edited by David Brower, Ballantine Books, New York. Especially good for mountain backpackers.

Outdoorsman's Handbook, Clyde Ormond, *Outdoor Life* and E.P. Dutton & Co., New York. Practical camping tips. Section of special interest to hunters. Helpful tips for horseback travel.

On Your Own in the Wilderness, Townsend Whelen and Bradford Angier, The Stackpole Company, Harrisburg, Pennsylvania. Packed with camping know-how.

Camping and Woodcraft, Horace Kephart, The Macmillan Company, New York. A 1917 update of a 1906 classic on the outdoors. Delightful winter reading for the summer camper, although there have been changes in outdoor living since Kephart trekked the wilderness.

The Golden Guide to Camping, Robert E. Smallman, Golden Press, New York. Lots of useful information in a pocket-size manual.

Camping Today, S. Blackwell Duncan, Rand McNally, Chicago, New York, San Francisco. Perhaps the most valuable book on our list for beginning family campers. An up-to-date discussion of our use of the outdoors with the family in mind. A helpful book list and addresses of national parks and trail systems.

Backpacking

Most of the books listed above discuss backpacking. Here are titles that go into deeper detail for families with special interest in trail trips on foot.

Lightweight Backpacking, Charles L. Jansen, Bantam Books, New York. Concise, reliable information for lightweight backpacking. The subtitle is "Two Cups, Two Spoons, Two Pots."

Home in Your Pack, Bradford Angier, Stackpole Books, Harrisburg, Pennsylvania. Angier is always delightful to read, and trustworthy.

The Man Who Walked Through Time, Collin Fletcher, Alfred A. Knopf, New York. One of our best-known hikers. This book is a case history of a hike through the Grand Canyon. We don't care for his theology, but Fletcher is a skilled camper.

Backpacking Made Easy, Michael Abel, Naturegraph Publishers, Healdsburg, California. A first-person account of packing adventures.

Many other titles could be listed, but these will give you a start. Check your library for camping and backpacking books.

Camp Cooking

Pleasant meals are entirely possible under the most primitive conditions, especially with the new processed camp foods. Supermarket shelves contain a wide variety of easily prepared, lightweight foods that are much less expensive than the packaged trail foods.

NOLS Cookery, Nancy Pallister: Editor, National Outdoor Leadership School, Lander, Wyoming. Nutrition and energy for lightweight backpackers. A booklet for every pack.

Food for Knapsackers and Other Trail Travelers, Hasse Bunnelle, A Sierra Club Totebook. This, along with *Cooking for Camp and Trail,* also a Totebook, belongs in the serious camper's library.

Coping with Camp Cooking, Mae Webb Stephens and George S. Wells, Stackpole Books, Harrisburg, Pennsylvania. Cooking on RV trips and general camping expeditions. Most helpful book with cookable recipes.

Simple Foods for the Pack, Vikki Kinmont and Claudia Axcell, Sierra Club Books, San Francisco, California. Unusual approach to camp cooking, especially for the trail camper. Natural foods are featured.

Wilderness Cookery, Bradford Angier, Stackpole Books, Harrisburg, Pennsylvania. A standard outdoor cooking book. Lots of how-to along with plain recipes. Good chapter on wild foods.

The Complete Outdoor Cookbook, Dan and Inez Morris, Hawthorn Books, New York. Everything you need to know about cooking outdoors, whether on the patio or along a trail. Good discussion of camp stoves.

Canoe Camping

We will resist allowing our bias to show through in our list of canoe camping titles. Your library and bookstore will offer many more.

North America Canoe Country, Calvin Rutstrum, Macmillan, New York. For the romance of canoeing and the historic canoe trips, read Rutstrum's book. It's a classic.

Introduction to Canoeing, Bradford Angier and Zack Taylor, Stackpole Books, Harrisburg, Pennsylvania. Clear instructions for the novice. A thorough discussion of all aspects of canoe travel.

The Canoe Camper's Handbook, Ray Bearse, Winchester Press, New York. The book for the serious canoe camper. Thorough discussion of canoeing along with a carefully documented where-to-go section. Get this book if you plan frequent canoe trips.

Miscellaneous Camping Books

The Complete Snow Camper's Guide, Raymond Bridge, Charles Scribner's Sons, New York. All about winter camping and travel. Good resource list for equipment, supplies and further reading.

Outdoorman's Fitness and Medical Guide, Lawrence Galton, *Outdoor Life* Harper & Row, New York. Health, nutrition, safety and first aid for outdoor living. Helpful.

Nature Oriented Activities, Betty Van Der Smissen and Oswald H. Goering, Iowa State University Press, Ames, Iowa. This is a leader's guide to outdoor activity for youth and adults. An invaluable book for parents who wish to make the outdoors a vital part of family experience. Thorough bibliographies. Clear instructions for nature crafts and collections, games, discovery activities, outdoor living skills.

Knots and How to Tie Them, Boy Scouts of America, New Brunswick, New Jersey. Just what the title says and more. All about rope and knots, how to tie them and where to use them.

Nature Recreation, William Gould, Vinal Dover Publications, New York. Group guidance for the out-of-doors. A host of ideas for outdoor learning and pleasure.

Living Off the Country, Bradford Angier, Stackpole Books, Harrisburg, Pennsylvania. Another Angier classic for pleasant reading and useful, potentially life-saving ideas. Wilderness survival is discussed in several new books. This will lay a foundation for continuing reading to those with special interests in this field of thought.

Field Guides

Identifying birds, trees, stars, rocks, and flowers intrigues millions of outdoor enthusiasts. Here are some identification guides we have found useful. There are several more you will discover in your reading and browsing in book stores.

Peterson Field Guide Series, Roger Tory Peterson, Editor; Houghton Mifflin Company, Boston. The guide series includes 21 titles widely recognized for ease of use and reliability. Topics covered are Birds, Shells, Butterflies, Mammals, Rocks and Minerals, Animal Tracks, Ferns, Trees and Shrubs, Reptiles and Amphibians, Wildflowers, Insects, Bird's Nests. Several topics are treated by regions. The identification system is simple to follow allowing anyone to correctly name the species of plant, animal, or mineral under study.

Golden Field Guide, Golden Press, New York. Two volumes that will prove helpful: *Birds of North America,* and *Trees of North America.* Beautifully illustrated with keys for identification. The books cover the more common species the camper is likely to encounter.

Golden Nature Guide, Golden Press, New York. The colorful, popular paperback books that should be found in every home to generate outdoor interest. Less detailed than the Golden Field Guides, but an excellent point of beginning. Topics discussed in the guides include Birds, Flowers, Insects, Trees, Reptiles and Amphibians, Stars, Mammals, Seashores, Fishes, Fossils, Game Birds, Zoology, Weather, Sea Shells of the World, Rocks and Minerals, Butterflies and Moths, Nonflowering Plants, Insect Pests, Pond Life, Zoo Animals, Spiders. Thorough enough to aid in identification of most of the natural items the family will find.

Wilderness Pocket 'n Pak Library, Life Support Technology, Inc., Manning, Oregon. Five booklets in a tough plastic folder. Available singly. Wilderness Survival, Medical Aid in the

Wilderness, Poisonous Plants, and two booklets on Edible Plants.

Complete Field Guide to American Wildlife, Henry Hill Collins, Jr. Harper & Row, New York. More than 600 pages of detailed information to identify wildlife east of the Rockies and north of the 37th Parallel, plus 877 species found in the West and Deep South. Useful for the serious outdoors person.

The Long Journey

Overlanding, John Steele Gordon, Harper and Row, New York. How to explore the world on four wheels. Travel beyond the U.S.-Canadian borders. Valuable for those planning driving trips in outer lands.

The Milepost, Alaska Northwest Publishing Co., Anchorage, Alaska. When you plan to drive the Alaska Highway, this is the book to get. Updated annually.

Nature

Exploring Nature with Your Child, Dorothy Edward Shuttlesworth, Greystone Press, New York. An introduction to the environment and understanding of nature for the whole family. Fascinating reading and background for trips afield.

If wilderness travel interests you, Rutstrum's *Wilderness Route Finder* will stir your imagination. All about maps, compasses, sextants, and the myth of moss on the north side of the trees.

We have been enriched by the American Heritage *Book of Natural Wonders,* and the Reader's Digest *Joy of Nature.* The Life *Nature Library* and the *Audubon Nature Encyclopedia* own a place on our shelves. You must interpret some of these writings for the children, for these writings refer occasionally to the theory of evolution as the basis for life. But the photographs and text stir the imagination.

Many, many titles have been omitted in this listing, some of them probably superior to the books we have named. You will find books that speak to you in a special way, as we have. As you observe nature, you will find your Bible coming alive in new ways, for the Scriptures are filled with references to God's creation.

National, State, and Provincial Camping Information Sources

A letter addressed to these offices will bring you details about camping opportunities in state parks, along with official tourist information bulletins. Provincial offices will supply information concerning Canada's unequalled camping areas. Additional help can be secured by writing or phoning the Canadian Tourist Bureau in your nearest large city.

National

Federal Reservoirs: U.S. Corps of Engineers, Dept. of the Army, Washington, D.C. 20315

Indian Reservations: Bureau of Indian Affairs, U.S. Dept. of the Interior, Washington, D.C. 20240

National Forests: Forest Service, U.S. Dept. of Agriculture, Washington, D.C. 20240

National Parks: National Park Service, U.S. Dept. of the Interior, Washington, D.C. 20240

Wildlife Refuges: Fish and Wildlife Service, U.S. Dept. of the Interior, Washington, D.C. 20240

Individual States

Alabama: Department of Conservation, State Capitol, Montgomery, Ala. 36104

Alaska: Alaska Travel Division, Box 2391, Juneau, Alaska 99801

Arizona: Arizona Development Board, 1500 W. Jefferson St., Phoenix, Ariz. 85007

Arkansas: Publicity and Parks Commission, State Capitol, Little Rock, Ark. 72201

California: Division of Beaches and Parks, P.O. Box 2390, Sacramento, Calif. 95811

Colorado: Department of Public Relations, State Capitol, Denver, Colo. 80203

Connecticut: Parks and Forest Commission, State of Connecticut, Hartford, Conn. 06115

Delaware: State Park Commission, 3300 Faulkland Road, Wilmington, Del. 19808

District of Columbia: National Capital Region, National Park Service, 1100 Ohio Dr., S.W., Washington, D.C. 20242

Florida: Florida Park Service, 101 W. Gaines St., Tallahassee, Fla. 32301

Georgia: Department of State Parks, 7 Hunter St., S.W., Atlanta, Ga. 30334

Hawaii: Division of State Parks, State of Hawaii, P.O. Box 621, Honolulu, Hawaii 96809

Idaho: Department of Commerce and Development, State House, Boise, Idaho 83720

Illinois: Illinois Division of Parks and Memorials, 100 State Office Bldg., Springfield, Ill. 62706

Indiana: Division of State Parks, 16 State Office Bldg., Indianapolis, Ind. 46209

Iowa: State Conservation Commission, East 7th and Court Ave., Des Moines, Iowa 50309

Kansas: State Park and Resources Authority, 801 Harrison, Topeka, Kan. 66612

Kentucky: Travel Division, Dept. of Public Information, Capitol Annex Bldg., Frankfort, Ky. 40601

Louisiana: State Parks and Recreation Commission, Old State Capitol Bldg., Baton Rouge, La. 70821

Maine: State Park and Recreation Commission, State House Office Bldg., Augusta, Me. 04330

Maryland: Department of Forests and Parks, State Office Bldg., Annapolis, Md. 21404

Massachusetts: Division of Parks and Forests, 15 Ashburton Pl., Boston, Mass. 02108

Michigan: Michigan Tourist Council, Stevens T. Mason Bldg., Lansing, Mich. 48926

Minnesota: Division of State Parks, 320 Centennial Office Bldg., St. Paul, Minn. 55101

Mississippi: State Park System, 1102 Woolfolk Bldg., Jackson, Miss. 39201

Missouri: State Park Board, 1206 Jefferson Bldg., Jefferson City, Mo. 65102

Montana: Montana Highway Commission, Helena, Mont. 59601

Nebraska: Nebraska Game, Forestation and Parks Commission, State Capitol, Lincoln, Neb. 68509

Nevada: State Park System, Carson City, Nev. 89701

New Hampshire: Division of Economic Development, State House Annex, Concord, N.H. 03301

New Jersey: Dept. of Conservation and Economic Development, P.O. Box 1889, Trenton, N.J. 08625

New Mexico: State Tourist Div., 302 Galisteo, Santa Fe, N.M. 87501

New York: Division of State Parks, State Campus Site, Albany, N.Y. 12226

North Carolina: Travel Information Div., Dept. of Conservation & Development, Raleigh, N.C. 27602

North Dakota: North Dakota Travel Dept., State Capitol, Bismarck, N.D. 58501

Ohio: Division of Parks and Recreation, 1500 Dublin Rd., Columbus, Ohio 43212

Oklahoma: Div. of State Parks, Rm. 533, State Capitol Bldg., Oklahoma City, Okla. 73105

Oregon: State Highway Dept., Salem, Ore. 97310

Pennsylvania: State Dept. of Forests and Waters, Harrisburg, Pa. 17120

Rhode Island: Rhode Island Development Council, Roger Williams Bldg., Hayes St., Providence, R.I. 02908

South Carolina: South Carolina Development Bd., Columbia, S.C. 29202

South Dakota: Dept. of Game, Fish and Parks, Pierre, S.D. 57501

Tennessee: Division of State Parks, 235 Cordell Hull Bldg., Nashville, Tenn. 37219

Texas: Texas State Parks Board, Drawer E, Capitol Station, Austin, Tex. 78701

Utah: Tourist and Publicity Council, State Capitol, Salt Lake City, Utah 84114

Vermont: Department of Forests and Parks, Montpelier, Vt. 05601

Virginia: Division of Public Relations and Advertising, 811 State Office Bldg., Richmond, Va. 23219

Washington: Parks and Recreation Commission, 522 S. Franklin, Olympia, Wash. 98502

West Virginia: Division of Parks and Recreation, State Office Bldg., Charleston, W. Va. 25305

Wisconsin: Vacation and Travel Service, Box 450, Madison, Wis. 53701

Wyoming: Travel Commission, 2320 Capitol Ave., Cheyenne, Wyo. 82001

Provincial

Alberta: Government Travel Bureau, 331 Highways Bldg., Edmonton, Alta.

British Columbia: Government Travel Bureau, Parliament Bldg., Victoria, B.C.

Manitoba: Bureau of Travel and Publicity, Legislative Bldg., Winnipeg, Man.

New Brunswick: Travel Bureau, 196 Queen St., Fredericton, N.B.

Newfoundland: Tourist Development Office, St. John's, Nfld.

Nova Scotia: Nova Scotia Travel Bureau, Halifax, N.S.

Ontario: Dept. of Tourism, 67 College St., Toronto, Ont.

Prince Edward Island: Travel Bureau, P.O. Box 1087, Charlottetown, P.E.I.

Quebec: Dept. of Tourism, 12 Ste. Anne St., Quebec, P.Q.

Saskatchewan: Tourist Development Branch, Power Bldg., Regina, Sask.

Yukon Territory: Department of Travel and Publicity, Whitehorse, Y.T.

National Park and Forest Information

More than 300 million acres of public lands await family campers in the U.S. and Canada, including some of the most magnificent wilderness areas of the world. Whether you plan a trail trip or an auto travel trek, you will want to enjoy the national and provincial camping areas.

A wide variety of publications related to camping can be obtained from:

Superintendent of Documents
U.S. Government Printing Office
Washington, D.C. 20402

You may write for a free listing of available publications. Be sure to specify your interests, such as the area you would like to visit and the type of camping or outdoor sport you are interested in.

The following publications are recommended and can be ordered from the Superintendent of Documents:

Backpacking in the National Forest Wilderness: A Family Adventure. 15¢

Camping in the National Park System. A guide to fees, facilities, etc. 25¢

Camping: Outdoors Calling You? A Forest Service booklet. 20¢

National Forest Vacations. A Forest Service booklet. 45¢

National Forest Wilderness and Primitive Areas. Map of 88 wilderness areas in 14 states. 15¢

National Park System Maps

National Parks, Historical Sites, and National Monuments.

National Wildlife Refuges. 35¢

Reclamation's Recreational Opportunities. 25¢

Room to Roam. A recreation guide to the public lands of the West. 75¢